Restoring God's Church to Holiness and Glory

Dallas Wauson

ISBN 979-8-89043-605-4 (paperback)
ISBN 979-8-89043-606-1 (digital)

Christian Faith Publishing
832 Park Avenue
Meadville, PA 16335
www.christianfaithpublishing.com

Printed in the United States of America

*Husbands, love your wives, just as Christ also loved the church
and gave Himself for her, that He might sanctify and cleanse her
with the washing of water by the word, that He might present her
to Himself a glorious church, not having spot or wrinkle or any
such thing, but that she should be holy and without blemish.*
—Ephesians 5:25–27

Contents

Foreword

I had the privilege of getting to know Pastor Dallas Wauson for the last few years of his life. During his transition from pastor to author, the Wausons relocated to Corpus Christi, Texas, and attended our church, New Life.

I am grateful for the time we had together. In every meeting we had, he would talk about revival. Every time he talked about revival, there was a tangible presence of the Holy Spirit along with tears and trembling. Pastor Dallas never lost his hunger for the move of God. And he never lost his love for the local church—a rare trait after four decades of ministry.

In our final meeting, he encouraged me and prayed over me. I am confident I received a blessing that day and I'm thankful for his impartation. I only wish I had known at the time that the meeting would be our last.

Not long after that meeting, Pastor Dallas went home to meet Jesus face-to-face and received his eternal reward. I told his wife, Colleen, that I believe I was one of Pastor Dallas's final assignments.

This book is also one of those final assignments. I believe as you read the truth contained in these pages, you will receive a similar impartation.

A primary theme seen throughout this book is the message of repentance. The American church is in desperate need of this message. Our culture is aggressively dark, immoral, godless, and adversarial toward the truth of the gospel. That culture is seeping into the next generation of Christianity.

In response, God is raising watchmen like Pastor Dallas to sound the alarm and bring a great spiritual awakening to America once again. My prayer is that you will not only receive this call to repentance on a personal level but you will also make this your own life message as you walk out the Great Commission in this last-day generation.

Pastor Zane Sturm
New Life Church
Corpus Christi, Texas

Preface

The following pages of this book are from a deep desire in the heart of Jehovah God to restore His Church. God speaks to His children in many ways. A Baptist pastor by the name of Martin Luther King spoke of a dream he had that was a call for love and unity among the people of this nation, the United States of America. Yes, he was also a civil rights activist, but even this desire came from a heart of love and not destruction. He remains famous for his "I Have a Dream" speech and the book he wrote outlining his dream. His dream cost him his life.

I, too, had a dream that I know was from God. In fact, it was not just one occurrence, but over a year, I had this same dream multiple times. At first, this dream was unexplainable because I am a nondenominational pastor with forty years' experience, and I could not understand why God was showing me this dream.

The dream was simple. My wife, Colleen, and I walked up to a building that could be used as a church in any town in America or any place in the world. From the outside, the building had an attraction that made you think it was a building that was being used as a church. Once you opened the door, the inside of the building was in disarray, with all kinds of trash and debris covering the floor. It was cold and dusty, with a dim light to reveal the condition. I looked at the light, and it was not a physical light. It was an ember with a flame of fire setting on it. I could sense the presence of God inside.

I pondered the dream for several weeks before I shared it with my wife. After our initial discussion and prayers, we still could not figure out what to do with the building. In each dream, the outside of the buildings were different sizes, but inside, the mess was the same—in disarray and ruin!

Finally, on October seventh of the year 2022, I had the dream once again. This time, I was meditating when God spoke, by His Holy Spirit, the reason for the dream. He said, "This is My Church, the Body of My son Jesus Christ, and it lies in ruins. I want you to declare My Holy Word to restore My church." The response in my mind was, *But how?*

The Spirit immediately spoke and said, "I gave you a gift to write. I want you to write what I will show you." But how could I spread the Word of God to Christians around the world? Once again, the Spirit spoke. "By being obedient to God."

So here is where I begin. I've already written one book titled *The Way of Escape from the Darkness*. This book was released on December 8, 2022. It was published by Christian Faith Publishing in Meadville, Pennsylvania. It is available in multiple bookstores around the world, including Amazon and Barnes and Noble.

Without the Holy Spirit, I could not write a book such as this because I do not know the heart of each one of God's children. However, there seems to be a universal thread that runs through Christians that allow themselves to not follow Jesus like they should. They are not led by the Holy Spirit like God has required. There is no power, or very little power, represented in the church today. It's important that we discover what this universal thread is and where it is rooted. Then we can repair the ruins, and healing will come. Remember, God is serious about rebuilding His Church. The Fire of God is still burning in His Church, and the "gates of hell will not prevail against it." This is the Church God will present to the Bridegroom that is "without spot or wrinkle!"

So prayerfully, I step forward to obey God's will in this matter and fulfill my purpose. Please do not receive this writing as a rebellious attack against different churches, denominations, or Christians around the world. This book is from the heart of God, who loves His Church and His Children. Love is still the key to healing all hurt in His Church. God's desire is to see His Church as a power-filled group of His people doing great things: signs and wonders, miracles, healing broken hearts, and gathering the fruit from the "fields that are white unto harvest!" Prayerfully, read and be sensitive to what God may show you or call you to do.

> *And He (Jesus) is the head of the body, the church, who is the beginning, the firstborn from the dead, that in all things He may have the preeminence.* (Colossians 1:18)

Let's help rebuild God's Church, which is one church—Jesus as the Head of God's Church and we as the Body of God's Church!

Chapter 1

An Overview of God's Church

God's purpose in creating His Church had many different reasons. God, in His infinite wisdom, could see a body of people with Christ as their head filling the world with a tremendous harvest.

> *For God so loved the world that He gave His only begotten Son, that whoever believes in Him should not perish but have everlasting life. For God did not send His Son into the world to condemn the world, but that the world through Him might be saved.* (John 3:16–17)

That is a picture of God's love for you and me.

Jesus, as a boy, had come to understand this purpose of His Heavenly Father at an early age. This story is important because it points not only the way for Jesus to walk, but what would transpire at the end of his ministry.

His parents went to Jerusalem every year at the Feast of the Passover. And when He was twelve years old, they went up to Jerusalem according to the custom of the feast. When they had finished the days, as they returned, the Boy Jesus lingered behind in Jerusalem. And Joseph and His mother did not know it; but supposing Him to have been in the company, they went a day's journey and sought Him among their relatives and acquaintances.

So when they did not find Him, they returned to Jerusalem, seeking Him. Now it was after three days they found Him in the temple, sitting in the midst of the teachers, both listening to them and asking them questions. And all who heard Him were astonished at His understanding and answers. So when they saw Him, they were amazed; and His mother said to Him:

> *"Son, why have You done this to us? Look, your father and I have sought You anxiously."*
> *And He said to them, "Why did you seek Me? Did you not know that I must be about My Father's business?" But they did not understand the statement which He spoke to them. (Luke 2:48–49)*

During the ministry of Jesus, God prophesied the start of His Church as Jesus spoke to Peter.

> *He said to them, "But who do you say that I am?"*
> *Simon Peter answered and said, "You are the Christ, the Son of the living God."*
> *Jesus answered and said to him, "Blessed are you, Simon Bar-Jonah, for flesh and blood has not revealed this to you, but My Father who is in heaven. And I also say to you that you are Peter, and on this rock, I will build My church, and the gates of Hades shall not prevail against it. And I will give you the keys of the kingdom of heaven, and whatever you bind on earth will be bound in heaven, and whatever you loose on earth will be loosed in heaven." (Matthew 16:15–19)*

> *Thomas said to Him, "Lord, we do not know where You are going, and how can we know the way?"*
> *Jesus said to him, "I am the way, the truth, and the life. No one comes to the Father except through Me." (John 14:5–6)*

This one scripture is extremely powerful when you understand what Jesus is saying. He was talking to Thomas (doubting Thomas) and was telling him a truth that still applies to every born-again Christian from the time of their new birth until today! Here is where "your awakening" begins. Why is this so important to us today? Why is it so important to us today that God restored His church? Why do we need to come to a fresh understanding of this scripture that Jesus spoke to Thomas?

Throughout the gospels, Jesus gathered disciples and followers unto Himself. He taught them about the Kingdom of God, about God's Church, and the Holy Spirit. He demonstrated the power of God in the gospel of Jesus Christ by ministering in healing and deliverance, in the power of prayer, and even raising the dead. He taught about the love of God and that we were supposed to walk daily in that love. He taught us about obedience and how rebellion could destroy our lives. He taught us to follow Him for He was the way out of the darkness. This was the first sign that reality had invaded the earth, and it came from heaven.

Before the death of Jesus, He anointed twelve disciples—and later, seventy-two disciples—with the power of the Kingdom of God. He told them to go forth and preach the gospel, with signs and wonders that would follow them. These men operated under the anointing that Jesus poured out on them. Later, they would be born again and filled with the Holy Spirit in the book of Acts.

After the death, burial, and resurrection of Jesus, He ascended into heaven. The Spirit of God was poured out upon all followers of Jesus in the upper room in Jerusalem. They experienced a dramatic change and went into the streets declaring the goodness of God. Out of this group of followers, God's Church would be established. The Church would begin to grow and prosper.

> *And they continued steadfastly in the apostles'*
> *doctrine and fellowship, in the breaking of bread,*
> *and in prayers. Then fear came upon every soul,*
> *and many wonders and signs were done through the*
> *apostles. Now all who believed were together, and*

had all things in common, and sold their possessions and goods, and divided them among all, as anyone had need.

So, continuing daily with one accord in the temple, and breaking bread from house to house, they ate their food with gladness and simplicity of heart, praising God and having favor with all the people. And the Lord added to the church daily those who were being saved. (Acts 2:42–47)

Years later, the church went through a time of persecution at the hands of a man named Saul. Yet God's grace and mercy enabled the church to survive. One day, on the road to Damascus, Saul is confronted by Jesus, and Saul gave his life to the Lord. After that, he was called Paul. He became an active Apostle and is credited with writing thirteen of the New Testament books.

Then the churches throughout all Judea, Galilee, and Samaria had peace and were edified; and walking in the fear of the Lord and in the comfort of the Holy Spirit, they were multiplied. (Acts 9:31)

God had in mind a perfect church to demonstrate His Kingdom here on earth. However, throughout history, we have not seen the church of God demonstrating the heart and the power of God here on earth. A few men and women have walked in the anointing down through history. A few outpourings have occurred but not the measure God intended. The truth is that when God starts a fire, He intends for it to spread. The church has never fully caught that vision. The writer of Proverbs describes this mindset perfectly.

There is a way that seems right to a man, but its end is the way of death. (Proverbs 14:12)

We have allowed the ways of the world (the flesh), the difficulties of this world, and our refusal to deal with our fleshly nature to rob us from receiving that fire! It is not God's fault; it is our fault! That is why we must repent and come back to the ways of God to see the church grow in a powerful, dynamic way. God wants His Church restored!

The letters in the New Testament are filled with reports of the new church of God. It also contains instructions on how they were to act in relationship with God and all churches. As the family of God in the twenty-first century, we should read and obey these instructions. Even though the instructions are over two thousand years old, we are still required to obey. These scriptures are our pathway as well, instructing us in the "Way of Jesus." We should walk and respond to God's instructions. In other words, we need to obey the word of God!

> *And do this, knowing the time, that now it is high time to awake out of sleep; for now, our salvation is nearer than when we first believed. The night is far spent; the day is at hand. Therefore, let us cast off the works of darkness, and let us put on the armor of light. Let us walk properly, as in the day, not in revelry (lively parties or festivities) and drunkenness, not in lewdness and lust, not in strife and envy. But put on the Lord Jesus Christ, and make no provision for the flesh, to fulfill its lusts.*
> (Romans 13:11–14)

This is a warning from God that not only spoke to the early church but is still truly relevant to us today! Part of the problem of the church being in ruins is that the people are engulfed in darkness. They are not walking with the Spirit of God, but they are caught up and in very much controlled by the world around them.

Many Christians today are caught up in all kinds of sin. Our lives are not a witness to the goodness and glory of God. The world is falling apart around us, and we continue business as usual, not paying any attention to the words of Jesus:

> *Watch and pray, lest you enter into temptation. The spirit indeed is willing, but the flesh is weak. (Matthew 26:41)*

> *But of that day and hour no one knows, not even the angels in heaven, nor the Son, but only the Father. Take heed, watch, and pray; for you do not know when the time is. (Mark 13:32–33)*

> *But take heed to yourselves, lest your hearts be weighed down with carousing, drunkenness, and cares of this life, and that Day come on you unexpectedly. For it will come as a snare on all those who dwell on the face of the whole earth. Watch therefore, and pray always that you may be counted worthy to escape all these things that will come to pass, and to stand before the Son of Man. (Luke 21:34–36)*

God is crying out through His Spirit, His Word, and to any of His children who will listen! There are signs all around us that we are in the beginning of the end-times. We can take the warning, repent, and turn our lives around to live like God requires. If not, we can suffer the consequences of disobeying God. These are the most serious times that the world has ever seen.

The Word of God continues to warn the people of God's Church. God used Paul the apostle to share the following warning.

> *For I have not shunned to declare to you the whole counsel of God. Therefore, take heed to yourselves and to all the flock, among which the Holy Spirit has made you overseers, to shepherd the church of God which He purchased with His own blood. For I know this, that after my departure sav-*

age wolves will come in among you, not sparing the flock. Also, from among yourselves men will arise, speaking perverse things, to draw away the disciples after themselves. Therefore, watch and remember that for three years I did not cease to warn everyone night and day with tears.

So now, brethren, I commend you to God and to the word of His grace, which can build you up and give you an inheritance among all those who are sanctified. (Acts 20:27–32)

Again, these words that Paul wrote are just as powerful and relevant to us today as when Paul wrote them!

Now I plead with you, brethren, by the name of our Lord Jesus Christ, that you all speak the same thing, and that there be no divisions among you, but that you be perfectly joined together in the same mind and in the same judgment.

For it has been declared to me concerning you, my brethren, by those of Chloe's household, that there are contentions among you.

Now I say this, that each of you says, "I am of Paul," or "I am of Apollos," or "I am of Cephas," or "I am of Christ." Is Christ divided? Was Paul crucified for you? Or were you baptized in the name of Paul? (1 Corinthians 1:10–13)

And I, brethren, when I came to you, did not come with excellence of speech or of wisdom declaring to you the testimony of God.

For I determined not to know anything among you except Jesus Christ and Him crucified.

I was with you in weakness, in fear, and in much trembling.

And my speech and my preaching were not with persuasive words of human wisdom, but in demonstration of the Spirit and of power, that your faith should not be in the wisdom of men but in the power of God. (1 Corinthians 2:1–5)

Where is the demonstration of the Spirit and of power in the church today? Many churches cannot answer this question. Where is the demonstration of power in individual Christians? Do you live and move in that power? Do you and Jesus walk together every day?

The reality of our generation has become the picture of sexual immorality in the world and, yes, even in the church. In the year 2022, it is even being taught in school systems to our children. Again, God warns the people of God and the church what will happen if they want to indulge in these sins and not repent!

It is reported that there is sexual immorality among you, and such sexual immorality as is not even named among the Gentiles, that a man has his father's wife! And you are puffed up, and have not rather mourned, that he who has done this deed might be taken away from among you. For I indeed, as absent in body but present in spirit, have already judged (as though I were present) him who has so done this deed. In the name of our Lord Jesus Christ, when you are gathered, along with my spirit, with the power of our Lord Jesus Christ, deliver such a one to Satan for the destruction of the flesh, that his spirit may be saved in the day of the Lord Jesus.

Your glorying is not good. Do you not know that a little leaven leavens the whole lump? Therefore, purge out the old leaven, that you may be a new lump, since you truly are unleavened. For indeed Christ, our Passover, was sacrificed for us. Therefore, let us keep the feast, not with old leaven, nor with the leaven of malice and wickedness, but with the unleavened bread of sincerity and truth. (1 Corinthians 5:1–8)

Paul says, "But now I have written to you not to keep company with anyone named a brother, who is sexually immoral, or covetous, or an idolater, or a reviler, or a drunkard, or an extortioner, not even to eat with such a person" (1 Corinthians 5:11).

That is strong language, but we know that God has called us to love everyone. We are to love them but not allow them to draw us into the power of temptation. The devil is still whispering in the ears of Christians, "Did God really say that we are not to associate with sinners?" He will use temptation in times you are weak to pull you into these same sins described in the above verse.

Looking at the church through generations past and looking at the generation today, we still have the same problems in the Church and in the lives of Christians. Is it no wonder that when God looks at His Church, He sees ruins and clutter? Not all Christians have gone offtrack, but there is enough to cause God to be concerned.

Now the Spirit expressly says that in latter times some will depart from the faith, giving heed to deceiving spirits and doctrines of demons, speaking lies in hypocrisy, having their own conscience seared with a hot iron. (1 Timothy 4:1–2)

We are seeing this in our nation right now! Everything has gone crazy, and the darkness has taken over! These are demonic forces who are attempting to destroy a Christian nation! Other nations have concerns as well. There must be a spiritual awakening of Christians to see a tremendous move of repentance take place in this hour. This is the reason for this book. Change is absolutely needed, and we must respond with our whole hearts.

Hunger and righteousness are the keys to revival! We need a strong sense of hunger and brokenness to draw us to the feet of Jesus and then allow repentance to flow. Repentance will bring restoration and holiness! Do you understand that the Church is not "like the world doing business as usual," but the Church must be "going about our Father's business in the kingdom of God"? Pray that God will give you a godly sorrow and convict your heart of sin and separation from Him and His Word. Then be about repentance and restoration in your own life.

Chapter 2

A Fresh New Beginning

We, as the worldwide body of Christ, need a fresh beginning in our commitment to Jesus. We need to go back to where we first met Jesus and examine our receiving Him as Lord and Savior, being baptized in water, and being filled with the Holy Spirit. If you are not confident in your early beginning with Jesus, come back to the Father with a repentant heart and ask Him to cleanse your heart of your sin.

We must walk in assurance of our salvation! If you believe you are saved, then you can start over by asking Jesus to show you the life you have lived. He can help renew your mind and "by the washing of the Word of God." Reality is found in the scripture below.

> *Therefore, if anyone is in Christ, he is a new creation; old things have passed away; behold, all things have become new. Now all things are of God, who has reconciled us to Himself through Jesus Christ, and has given us the ministry of reconciliation, that is, that God was in Christ reconciling the world to Himself, not imputing their trespasses to them, and has committed to us the word of reconciliation.*
>
> *Now then, we are ambassadors for Christ, as though God were pleading through us: we implore*

you on Christ's behalf, be reconciled to God. For He made Him who knew no sin to be sin for us, that we might become the righteousness of God in Him. (2 Corinthians 5:17–21)

I believe we can see this truth in the parable of the lost son. A father had two sons, and one decided he wanted his inheritance, so he went out on his own. The father complied, and the son left. However, things did not turn out well. On the verge of starvation and exhaustion, the son decided to repent and go back to his father's house. He returned to the place that he had moved away from and was now experiencing a repentant attitude. Look at how the father (who represents God) received the son on his return.

> *But when he came to himself, he said, "How many of my father's hired servants have bread enough and to spare, and I perish with hunger! I will arise and go to my father, and will say to him, 'Father, I have sinned against heaven and before you, and I am no longer worthy to be called your son. Make me like one of your hired servants.'"*
>
> *And he arose and came to his father. But when he was still a great way off, his father saw him and had compassion, and ran and fell on his neck and kissed him. And the son said to him, "Father, I have sinned against heaven and in your sight, and am no longer worthy to be called your son." But the father said to his servants, "Bring out the best robe and put it on him and put a ring on his hand and sandals on his feet. And bring the fatted calf here and kill it and let us eat and be merry; for this my son was dead and is alive again; he was lost and is found." And they began to be merry.* (Luke 15:17–24)

This is called reconciliation. This is available to those who know they have messed up and want to come back to God the Father.

Listen, it does not make any difference if your mistakes are big or small. Repentance is the way to reconcile with God. Repentance is the way to reconcile with anyone. I feel in my heart that God has called for His church to be restored. There are so many ways that we can fall short in our relationship with God because of our neglect in prayer, reading and focusing our thoughts on the Word of God, not being led by the Holy Spirit, and not living a life walking in the Kingdom of God. We have either ignored or we are ignorant of the way that God has called us to walk.

God had in mind a perfect church to demonstrate His Kingdom here on Earth. However, throughout history, we have not seen the church of God demonstrating the heart and the power of God here on Earth. We have seen historical moves of the Spirit that came down and swept through areas in America and other nations of the world, but these movements did not last.

Even churches in the history of the early church had instances of God's outpouring of fire, but they did not last. They withered away because Christian people did not nourish and keep the fire going! Let me say this again: "The truth is that when God starts a fire, He intends for it to spread." The church has never caught that vision. The writer of Proverbs describes this mindset perfectly.

*There is a way that seems right to a man, but
its end is the way of death.* (Proverbs 14:12)

The church is beginning to see a fresh outpouring of God's at the University of Asbury in Kentucky. The fire is spreading but will only continue as people pursue that fire and stoke it with the oil of the Holy Spirit! It takes a hunger to pursue revival!

We have allowed the ways of the world (the flesh), the difficulties of this world, and the refusal to deal with our fleshly nature to rob us from receiving and maintaining that fire! It Is not God's fault; it is our fault! That is why we must repent and come back to the ways of God so that we can see the church grow in a powerful, dynamic way! God wants His Church restored! We must submit ourselves to

Jesus as Lord and Savior in our lives once again and keep ourselves in His presence.

> *And He put all things under His feet and gave Him to be head over all things to the church, which is His body, the fullness of Him who fills all in all.* (Ephesians 1:22–23)

> *Husbands, love your wives, just as Christ also loved the church and gave Himself for her, that He might sanctify and cleanse her with the washing of water by the word, that He might present her to Himself a glorious church, not having spot or wrinkle or any such thing, but that she should be holy and without blemish.* (Ephesians 5:25–27)

Paul wrote that we are to be washed by the water of the Word of God. If we are not reading and meditating in God's word every day, then we cannot be sanctified and cleansed. The Church of God, the Body of Christ, "should be holy and without blemish." Out of the love Jesus has poured into our hearts, we ought to be sold out to holiness and purity! Holiness: how many of us can say, with a pure heart and a clear conscience, that we are holy?

Let me give you an example of what God revealed to me one day. In my spirit, I began to hear the music and lyrics of "The Battle Hymn of the Republic." I have heard this song all my life, and I even play it on the piano. This once was a poem written by Julia Ward Howe back in 1861, and the music is believed to be written by William Steffe. I will share with you a section of lines that spoke to my heart.

> *In the beauty of the lilies*
> *Christ was born across the sea*
> *With a glory in His bosom*
> *That transfigures you and me,*
> *As He died to make men holy*

And right here on the word "holy," God illuminated in my heart that I did not walk in holiness. What a shock and a wakeup call! I didn't hear the rest of the hymn because my heart was crying out for forgiveness and repentance. Holiness and purity are the heart of God that He wants to implant in our lives.

> *O Corinthians! We have spoken openly to you; our heart is wide open. You are not restricted by us, but you are restricted by your own affections. Now in return for the same (I speak as to children), you also be open. Do not be unequally yoked together with unbelievers. For what fellowship has righteousness with lawlessness? And what communion has light with darkness? And what accord has Christ with Belial? (In the New Testament, "Belial" means the devil.) Or what part has a believer with an unbeliever? And what agreement has the temple of God with idols? For you are the temple of the living God. As God has said:*
> *"I will dwell in them and walk among them. I will be their God, and they shall be My people."*
> *Therefore, come out from among them and be separate, says the Lord. Do not touch what is unclean, and I will receive you. I will be a Father to you, and you shall be My sons and daughters, says the Lord Almighty.* (2 Corinthians 6:11–18)

God is looking for repentance and purity.

> *Therefore, having these promises, beloved, let us cleanse ourselves from all filthiness of the flesh and spirit, perfecting holiness in the fear of God.* (2 Corinthians 7:1)

> *Furthermore, brethren, we urge and exhort in the Lord Jesus that you should abound more and*

more, just as you received from us how you ought to walk and to please God; for you know what commandments we gave you through the Lord Jesus.

For this is the will of God, your sanctification: that you should abstain from sexual immorality; that each of you should know how to possess his own vessel in sanctification and honor, not in passion of lust, like the Gentiles who do not know God; that no one should take advantage of and defraud his brother in this matter, because the Lord is the avenger of all such, as we also forewarned you and testified. For God did not call us to uncleanness, but in holiness. Therefore, he who rejects this does not reject man, but God, who has also given us His Holy Spirit. (1 Thessalonians 4:1–8)

For this reason we also, since the day we heard it, do not cease to pray for you, and to ask that you may be filled with the knowledge of His will in all wisdom and spiritual understanding; that you may walk worthy of the Lord, fully pleasing Him, being fruitful in every good work and increasing in the knowledge of God; strengthened with all might, according to His glorious power, for all patience and longsuffering with joy; giving thanks to the Father who has qualified us to be partakers of the inheritance of the saints in the light. He has delivered us from the power of darkness and conveyed us into the kingdom of the Son of His love, in whom we have redemption through His blood, the forgiveness of sins.

He is the image of the invisible God, the firstborn over all creation. For by Him all things were created that are in heaven and that are on earth, visible and invisible, whether thrones or dominions or principalities or powers. All things were created through Him and for Him. And He is before all things, and in Him all things consist of. And He is the head of the body, the church, who is the beginning, the firstborn from the dead, that in all things He may have the preeminence. (Colossians 1:9–18)

I write so that you may know how you ought to conduct yourself in the house of God, which is the church of the living God, the pillar and ground of the truth. And without controversy great is the mystery of godliness:
God was manifested in the flesh,
Justified in the Spirit,
Seen by angels,
Preached among the Gentiles,
Believed on in the world,
Received up in glory. (1 Timothy 3:15–16)

Hallelujah, Lord, show us your Glory!

There have been millions who have received Jesus Christ as their Lord and Savior over the last two thousand plus years. They did everything right when they received Jesus, and yet they fell back into life as usual. Often, the salvation experience was minimal in their lives. They found themselves returning to living the same life as it was before being saved. Somehow, this word from Paul never manifested in their lives.

Therefore, if anyone is in Christ, he is a new creation; old things have passed away; behold all things have become new. (2 Corinthians 5:17)

So Jesus says, "I am the way!" What does He mean? Is there a path or road that we are to follow after receiving salvation and the infilling of the Holy Spirit? Absolutely! Are you walking in the "way"? We will read more about this in chapter four. Right now would be a good place to pause and pray to ask God to forgive us for not walking in holiness and purity.

Prayer

Heavenly Father, I confess before you today that I have been seriously lacking in obeying the pathway that you have given me for my life. I ask that you forgive me for not taking it seriously and not walking in purity and holiness. I confess this is my sin before you and ask that you forgive me.

I also ask that you forgive me for not allowing the Holy Spirit to lead my life every day. (If you are not filled with the Holy Spirit, ask God to fill you.) Cleanse me from all my sin and deliver me from all rebellion against You and Your Word. I want to be reconciled to You, Father God. Thank you for my salvation and for placing me on the right pathway of life You bought and paid for on that cross. I pray this is the name of Jesus Christ.

Now let us continue in being prepared to raise up God's church out of the ruins and rubble.

Chapter 3

The Reality of God's Kingdom

For us to understand the restoration of God's Church, we must understand the reality of the Kingdom of God. It is something we need to concentrate and even study upon to see what Jesus was teaching in the early times of His ministry. Jesus was real then, and He is still real today! Heaven invaded the Earth through Jesus Christ!

> *In the beginning was the Word, and the Word was with God, and the Word was God. He was in the beginning with God. All things were made through Him, and without Him nothing was made that was made. In Him was life, and the life was the light of men. And the light shines in the darkness, and the darkness did not comprehend it.*
>
> *There was a man sent from God, whose name was John. This man came for a witness, to bear witness of the Light, that all through him might believe. He was not that Light but was sent to bear witness of that Light. That was the true Light which gives light to every man coming into the world.*
>
> *He was in the world, and the world was made through Him, and the world did not know Him. He came to His own, and his own did not receive Him. But as many as received Him, to them He*

gave the right to become children of God, to those who believe in His name: who were born, not of blood, nor of the will of the flesh, nor of the will of man, but of God.

And the Word became flesh and dwelt among us, and we beheld His glory, the glory as of the only begotten of the Father, full of grace and truth. John bore witness of Him and cried out, saying, "This was He of whom I said, 'He who comes after me is preferred before me, for He was before me.'" And of His fullness we have all received, and grace for grace. For the law was given through Moses, but grace and truth came through Jesus Christ. No one has seen God at any time. The only begotten Son, who is in the bosom of the Father, He has declared Him. (John 1:1–18)

Jesus came to proclaim the reality of God the Father and the Kingdom of God. He was on the Earth in a physical body, but He and the Father were still one. This connection was a new reality that was entering the Earth. The times were no longer the law in the Old Testament. God was introducing a new way of having a relationship with Him and His son Jesus. He prays for His disciples to see this reality. Jesus explains His relationship with the Old Testament law in the following verses.

Do not think that I came to destroy the Law or the Prophets. I did not come to destroy but to fulfill. For assuredly, I say to you, till heaven and earth pass away, one jot or one tittle will by no means pass from the law till all is fulfilled. Whoever therefore breaks one of the least of these commandments, and teaches men so, shall be called least in the kingdom of heaven; but whoever does and teaches them, he shall be called great in the kingdom of heaven. For I say to you, that unless your righteousness exceeds

the righteousness of the scribes and Pharisees, you will by no means enter the kingdom of heaven.
(Matthew 5:17–20)

The words of Jesus were for the Pharisees to hear, but to His disciples, they must understand and obey. Love is the key, and yet the church of God lacks in that love among many of the Christians. In my forty years in the pastoral ministry, I have seen many instances of backbiting, unforgiveness, hatred, and anger over simple little issues. Supposedly, Christian people get mad at the pastor, a layperson, or some other member, and they up and quit the church. Too many times, I have seen the lack of love in the very place that it should be abundant, and that is in the church.

Jesus said to him, "You shall love the Lord your God with all your heart, with all your soul, and with all your mind. This is the first and great commandment. And the second is like it: 'You shall love your neighbor as yourself.' On these two commandments hang all the Law and the Prophets."
(Matthew 22:37–40)

Love should be easy, but for those who practice living in the flesh nature, it is very difficult to love at times. That's why Jesus wants us to understand that we must learn how to live in the flesh but be obedient to the law of love in the Kingdom of God. We are to be led by the Spirit of God and not the flesh. Sounds difficult, but we can change by renewing our minds with the Word of God.

Owe no one anything except to love one another, for he who loves another has fulfilled the law. For the commandments, "You shall not commit adultery," "You shall not murder," "You shall not steal," "You shall not bear false witness," "You shall not covet," and if there is any other commandment, are all summed up in this saying, namely, "You shall love your neighbor as yourself." Love does no harm to a neighbor; therefore, love is the fulfillment of the law. (Romans 13:8–10).

For Christ is the end of the law for righteousness to everyone who believes. (Romans 10:4)

We need to be encouraged by the Word of God and even Jesus Himself! He explained about His disciples not being of this world just like He was not of this world. So He asked God the Father to sanctify those who believed in Him and who believed they could walk in the anointing. We are sanctified by the truth. Sanctified means to be set apart. We are not to look like the world or act like the world. Jesus himself has set us apart to carry forth the Kingdom of God.

But now I come to You, and these things I speak in the world, that they may have My joy fulfilled in themselves. I have given them Your word; and the world has hated them because they are not of the world, just as I am not of the world. I do not pray that You should take them out of the world, but that You should keep them from the evil one. They are not of the world, just as I am not of the world. Sanctify them by Your truth. Your word is truth. As You sent Me into the world, I also have sent them into the world. And for their sakes I sanctify Myself, that they also may be sanctified by the truth. (John 17:13–19)

Jesus made a very important and profound statement in His prayer for His disciples: "They are not of the world, just as I am not of the world." Is there something new and unusual going on in God's Kingdom here on earth?

I do not pray for these alone, but also for those who will believe in Me through their word; that they all may be one, as You, Father, are in Me, and I in You; that they also may be one in Us, that the world may believe that You sent Me. And the glory which You gave Me I have given them, that they may be one just as We are one: I in them, and You in Me; that they may be made perfect in one, and that the world may know that You have sent Me, and have loved them as You have loved Me.

Father, I desire that they also whom You gave Me may be with Me where I am, that they may behold My glory which You have given Me; for You loved Me before the foundation of the world. O righteous Father! The world has not known You, but I have known You; and these have known that You sent Me. And I have declared to them Your name, and will declare it, that the love with which You loved Me may be in them, and I in them. (John 17:20–26)

Here is one of the most powerful weapons that Christians and God's Church have that is yet to be established, and they would walk and become powerful in the world through "unity or being in one accord." We are to be in one accord with God, with Jesus Christ, with the Church of God, and with one another! Unity (*all of us agreeing together*) is the overcoming power that changes everything!

In His ministry, Jesus wanted not only His disciples to know, but the whole world to know, that He was not of this world. In fact, Jesus spoke this truth forty-one times throughout the gospels. This truth was hard for the disciples to receive and even harder for believers to receive in our current time in history. Apparently, some of the disciples in the early church believed what Jesus said, and they ministered like Jesus. They preached the gospel, laid hands on the sick and they recovered, they cast out demons, and healed the brokenness in people's lives.

Fantastic! Moving like Jesus in His reality here on this Earth. But what happened? Slowly, this deep belief in the words of Jesus somehow became shallow and, eventually, almost disappeared. Yes, throughout history, there had been men and women who believed and moved in the power of the Holy Spirit and brought an awareness to the world and the church. Yet there are still many who do not believe in the power of God working in the earthly realm and in earthly vessels.

Why is this so hard for us to discern two thousand years later? This is a major weakness in God's Church that we do not believe we are a part of God's Kingdom when we are saved, and that we can walk with the Holy Spirit just like Jesus and His disciples did. Most of our lives have been changed since we first believed, but we have allowed the devil to rob us of our inheritance. Our belief has been in words and not in action and power!

Listen, walking in the reality of the Kingdom of God is a daily, intimate walk with Jesus, trusting Him that you are not the "the old man" who was saved. You have become a new creation in Christ Jesus, yet the absence of daily fellowship, prayer, worship, and spending time listening to the Holy Spirit has blinded you to your real inheritance!

So who are we? We have believed so many people that have taught us to go in different directions! Who are we? Let's see what the Scripture says.

> *And you He made alive, who were dead in trespasses and sins, in which you once walked according to the course of this world, according to the prince of the power of the air, the spirit who now works in the sons of disobedience, among whom also we all once conducted ourselves in the lusts of our flesh, fulfilling the desires of the flesh and of the mind, and were by nature children of wrath, just as the others.*
>
> *But God, who is rich in mercy, because of His great love with which He loved us, even when we were dead in trespasses, made us alive together with Christ (by grace you have been saved), and raised us up together, and made us sit together in the heav-*

enly places in Christ Jesus, that in the ages to come He might show the exceeding riches of His grace in His kindness toward us in Christ Jesus. For by grace, you have been saved through faith, and that not of yourselves; it is the gift of God, not of works, lest anyone should boast. For we are His workmanship, created in Christ Jesus for good works, which God prepared beforehand that we should walk in them. (Ephesians 2:1–10)

Do you understand the words of Paul given to him by the Holy Spirit?

(God) made us alive together with Christ (by grace you have been saved), and raised us up together, and made us sit together in the heavenly places in Christ Jesus, that in the ages to come He might show the exceeding riches of His grace in His kindness toward us in Christ Jesus. (Ephesians 1:5–7)

How can you and I be seated in heavenly places in Christ Jesus if we don't believe that we have become a part of the Kingdom of God when we received salvation? Think about that!

Chapter 4

Walking in Reality

The purpose of this book is not to cause you to doubt your salvation, your baptism, and the life you have walked in Christ Jesus. If you are not sure you are saved, then find a Christian or the pastor of a church who can share the true gospel, the love of God, and the death of His Son Jesus, who died for your sins. Ask them to pray for you to receive Jesus and to be filled with the Holy Spirit.

The real purpose is to awaken the Body of Christ, which is the Church of God, to the reality that the world and the flesh has influenced our walk with Jesus and our relationship with Him. When we look at our life in Christ, almost always, we think that it means we are going to heaven when we die. We can live like we want to in the world, allowing the "lusts of the flesh, the lust of the eyes, and the boastful pride of life" to be our influence instead of the Word of God, prayer, being led by the Holy Spirit, and our intimate time of fellowship with our Heavenly Father. We think our worldly commitment is pleasing to God, but it's not!

However, God has looked at His Church over the years, and He doesn't see the way we see. God says, "His church is in ruins and rubble." Don't you think it is time to wake up and look at what God sees?

Do not love the world or the things in the
world. If anyone loves the world, the love of the

Father is not in him. For all that is in the world, the lust of the flesh, the lust of the eyes, and the boastful pride of life is not of the Father but is of the world. And the world is passing away, and the lust of it; but he who does the will of God abides forever. (1 John 2:15–17)

Here is the heart of God for the church! I will repeat it!

Husbands, love your wives, just as Christ also loved the church and gave Himself for her, that He might sanctify and cleanse her with the washing of water by the word, that He might present her to Himself a glorious church, not having spot or wrinkle or any such thing, but that she should be holy and without blemish. (Ephesians 5:25–28)

In the very beginning, when Jesus was talking and praying with His disciples, He explained very clearly why He was here, where He was going, and what would happen to Him in the end. These same words are for us today so that we can also hear God's plan for Jesus, God's Kingdom, and His plans for us today. Yet there is so much doubt in the lives of Christians and in our churches today. Let's examine a passage that clarifies who Jesus really is and why He came to earth.

I used a passage of scripture previously that I want to go back and clarify.

Thomas said to Him, "Lord, we do not know where You are going, and how can we know the way?"

Jesus said to him, "I am the way, the truth, and the life. No one comes to the Father except through Me." (John 14:5–6)

Have we become doubters like Thomas? If we really believed what Jesus spoke to Thomas, we would be right in the middle of the Kingdom of God and following Jesus daily. Let's look at what Jesus said in the above verse.

"I am the way." The word *way* indicates Jesus's ultimate declaration that Jesus is the only way to Father God. As Christians, many believe that truth. Yet in this twenty-first century, many don't believe what He said. They have created their own pathway to God and to heaven. They believe there are other ways to eternal life besides believing in Jesus, that He was the Son of God, and that He died on the cross for our sins because God loved us. They believe we can live a life of sin without repentance and go to heaven when we die. Some believe everybody goes to heaven when they die. However, because it is God's heaven, don't you think we need to follow His instructions?

Is there really a way? Well, Jesus said there was, and He never lies! So maybe, our doubt is because we don't understand what the "way" entails. This *way* begins at the time of our salvation when we are born again. We believe Jesus is the Son of God, that He died on a cross for our sins, that we are cleansed by His blood, and that He arose from the dead. Have you come that far?

Then Jesus explains the next step to His disciples to encourage them that there is a pathway to follow.

> *Then Jesus said to His disciples, "If anyone desires to come after Me, let him deny himself, and take up his cross, and follow Me. For whoever desires to save his life will lose it, but whoever loses his life for My sake will find it. For what profit is it to a man if he gains the whole world, and loses his own soul? Or what will a man give in exchange for his soul? For the Son of Man will come in the glory of His Father with His angels, and then He will reward each according to his works." (Matthew 16:24–27)*

In other words, deny yourself from seeking righteousness in your flesh and seek after purity and righteousness in Christ Jesus. Lay down your life and pick up your cross of daily denial and follow Jesus. It's not about you anymore, but it's all about Jesus and His Kingdom. You cannot save yourself!

Walking with Jesus requires obedience and intimacy and to be led by the Holy Spirit. Anything apart from that is a worldly view and a lie of the devil. You know the devil still lies, don't you?

Then Jesus says, "I am the truth." The word *truth* is the Greek word *aletheia*, and it means "reality." Jesus is saying, "I am going to lead you into the reality from which I came. I gave you life through My crucifixion so that you could also experience My life in the reality of the Kingdom of God. You can live on earth but walk in My Kingdom."

Truth on earth is rapidly becoming obsolete. There are so many people who are liars in the world today, and there is no sign of change. There is so much evidence of lying in our world leaders, our national leaders, including the United States, and in every walk of life! Lying seems to be a way of life! That is why Jesus wants us to understand that His life is founded in truth or reality. When Jesus tells you something, it is real! That is why we should strive to read the scriptures in the Bible and ask the Holy Spirit to teach us the Word of God.

Evangelist and president of Oral Roberts University in Tulsa, Oklahoma, had a favorite declaration. "See the invisible, and do the impossible." This is what reality in the Kingdom of God and the reality that Jesus said we could walk in is all about. It's called renewing our mind from thinking like the world and beginning to think according to the ways of God's Kingdom. The world's reality is "you get what you see, and you are stuck with it."

The founder of the Salvation Army, William Booth, is well-known for a profound statement he would make many times. He said, "I am not waiting for a move of God; I am a move of God!" This is what Jesus was talking about. This is a vital DNA of a disciple of Jesus that is captured in this statement. Are you a move of God?

Then Jesus said, "I am the life." Think about that statement. If we were not educated in the Word of God, we could assume that

Jesus meant everything He did on Earth. He was not finished living life on earth or in heaven. Jesus tells us the real story in verse below.

> *So then, after the Lord had spoken to them, He was received up into heaven, and sat down at the right hand of God. And they went out and preached everywhere, the Lord working with them and confirming the word through the accompanying signs. Amen. (Mark 16:19–20)*

"The Lord working with them." Doesn't sound like He abandoned His disciples, does it? He has not abandoned us either! Jesus lives within each Christian, and Jesus is the Head of God's Church. I can't explain that, but He is. He is always walking with us and working alongside us. Do you understand that? The life of Jesus is a Kingdom way of life. It has no beginning, and it has no end.

> *Now it was the Feast of Dedication in Jerusalem, and it was winter. And Jesus walked in the temple, in Solomon's porch. Then the Jews surrounded Him and said to Him, "How long do You keep us in doubt? If you are the Christ, tell us plainly."*
>
> *Jesus answered them, "I told you, and you do not believe. The works that I do in My Father's name, bear witness of Me. But you do not believe, because you are not of My sheep, as I said to you. My sheep hear My voice, and I know them, and they follow Me. And I give them eternal life, and they shall never perish; neither shall anyone snatch them out of My hand. My Father, who has given them to Me, is greater than all; and no one is able to snatch them out of My Father's hand. I and My Father are one." (John 10:22–30)*

Do you see the greatness of the love of God for each one of us as His child? There is intimacy on every front. Jesus says that we can hear His voice. Not necessarily an audible voice, but a whisper or a leading in our spirit. He is instructing us the way to follow Him. He is the Good Shepherd!

He has given us eternal life, and no one can take us away from Jesus except ourselves. We are the ones that need to make that daily denial of ourselves and follow Jesus wherever He leads. We are the ones who need to seek that daily fellowship with Him through prayer and spending time in His presence. We are the ones who are to strive to enter through the narrow gate and stay on the pathway.

> *And He said to them, "Strive to enter through the narrow gate, for many, I say to you, will seek to enter and will not be able. When once the Master of the house has risen up and shut the door, and you begin to stand outside and knock at the door, saying, 'Lord, Lord, open for us,' and He will answer and say to you, 'I do not know you, where you are from,' then you will begin to say, 'We ate and drank in Your presence, and You taught in our streets.' But He will say, 'I tell you I do not know you, where you are from. Depart from Me, all you workers of iniquity.'*
>
> *There will be weeping and gnashing of teeth, when you see Abraham and Isaac and Jacob and all the prophets in the kingdom of God, and yourselves thrust out. They will come from the east and the west, from the north and the south, and sit down in the kingdom of God. And indeed, there are last who will be first, and there are first who will be last."*
> (Luke 13:23–30)

These are the kind of verses we like to overlook or say that we don't understand and try not to find the truth. Whether we accept the truth of Jesus or not, we will still be held accountable on the day of judgment. Our rejection and denial will be the source of our missing entry into God's heaven. Do you understand that?

Jesus was cruelly beaten, hung on a cross, died, and was buried for us and our sin! Yet He was raised from the dead, and He declared His victory over sin and the grave so that by believing in Him we might have eternal life! Denying, or not accepting the truth of God's Word, is part of the rubble and ruins that God sees in His Church! Why can't we follow Him through the "narrow gate" and follow His way every day? It all comes down to our love, our obedience, and our hunger for purity.

God is not condemning churches all over the world! He is calling them to repentance and a submission to what His Word teaches about His Church. We have so many denominational churches, churches based and rooted in doctrines and traditions, and churches founded on men's interpretations and other extreme teachings. No wonder God is concerned! There are beliefs around the world that are founded on different gods, and they all teach that there is a hereafter. Confusion and lies have caused many people to miss God's intention of eternal salvation!

Many people are in dire distress in their beliefs and need the truth to change their lives. As Christians dedicated to the reality and fullness of God, we can minister that truth to them. We can agree with God and do our part to help restore and raise up God's Church out of the rubble and ruins! Can you see what God is calling you to individually do at this time and place? We can work with God to restore His Church and gain a future that will be in Him!

Right now, here in the United States of America, we have over two hundred million people who confess that they are Christians. Can you imagine the impact we can have on the whole world in working with God to reach the masses for Christ? We can if we stand up and agree with God and see the church raised up mighty in strength and power! We can if we believe that God wants us to be His Church "without spot or wrinkle."

For the kingdom of God is not in word but in power. (1 Corinthians 4:20–21)

> *For our gospel did not come to you in word only, but also in power, and in the Holy Spirit and in much assurance, as you know what kind of men, we were among you for your sake"* (1 Thessalonians 1:5)

Oh, that we would awaken to the Word of God and the Power of God and watch the harvest of the world take place! The truth that Jesus spoke to His disciples is the same truth He is speaking to us today.

> *Then He said to His disciples, "The harvest truly is plentiful, but the laborers are few. Therefore, pray to the Lord of the harvest to send out laborers into His harvest."* (Matthew 9:37–38)

Chapter 5

Stepping into the Restoration

Hopefully by now we have a clear vision of what needs to be done. God could move upon the church by Himself and bring restoration, but we might not enjoy what we would have to go through. I believe God wants us to restore the church, but how can we take on such a massive project? God is a God of restoration, and He has used His people to accomplish restorations in the Old Testament.

Let's study a little history and find out just how God can work through a large amount of people. Remember, what was done in the Old Testament was a restoration of a city made of stones, bricks, and timbers. Our task is going to be in rebuilding the hearts of Christian people worldwide. Pulling people out of fleshly deception and delivering them into restoration of their lives in Christ!

Let's go back into the Old Testament to the book of Nehemiah. I love this story because it tells us what God can do with a group of fifty thousand people and what the people can do that are dedicated to the Lord God to complete the task.

Nehemiah was the person that God would use to do a massive work of restoration in the city of Jerusalem. He was not some well-known man, yet he had a job in the presence of the king. Nehemiah was the king's cupbearer. His job was to ensure that the wine offered to the king had not been poisoned. He was the kind of man that Jesus would describe later in history.

> *Greater love has no one than this, than to lay down one's life for his friends.* (John 15:13)

Nehemiah spoke, in his own words, about the preliminary events that came and would change his life. It could even put his life in jeopardy.

> *The words of Nehemiah the son of Hachaliah. It came to pass in the month of Chislev, in the twentieth year, as I was in Shushan the citadel, that Hanani, one of my brethren, came with men from Judah; and I asked them concerning the Jews who had escaped, who had survived the captivity, and concerning Jerusalem. And they said to me, "The survivors who are left from the captivity in the province are there in great distress and reproach. The wall of Jerusalem is also broken down, and its gates are burned with fire." So it was, when I heard these words, that I sat down and wept, and mourned for many days; I was fasting and praying before the God of heaven.* (Nehemiah 1:1–4)

Here is a man who was living a good life, and when he heard the reports of his friends about the city of Jerusalem, it devastated him. He loved Jerusalem like God loved this same city. Jerusalem was the city that God had said He had chosen as a dwelling place for His name. It was the same with Jesus and the Church. So Nehemiah reminds God of His promise to these servants as well as himself.

> *Remember, I pray, the word that You commanded Your servant Moses, saying, "If you are unfaithful, I will scatter you among the nations; but if you return to Me, and keep My commandments*

and do them, though some of you were cast out to the farthest part of the heavens, yet I will gather them from there, and bring them to the place which I have chosen as a dwelling for My name." Now these are Your servants and Your people, whom You have redeemed by Your great power, and by Your strong hand. O Lord, I pray, please let Your ear be attentive to the prayer of Your servant, and to the prayer of Your servants who desire to fear Your name; and let Your servant prosper this day, I pray, and grant him mercy in the sight of this man. For I was the king's cupbearer. (Nehemiah 1:8–11)

Nehemiah had a cushy but risky job, seated at the king's table, and Nehemiah's countenance was sad. This was a dangerous attitude that could cost him his job and maybe even his life. Yet during this situation, God was at work, calling Nehemiah to do a task for Him and would even supply everything he would need to finish the project. During and after this encounter with the King, Nehemiah continued to pray and fast, calling out to God in repentance for his own sin and the sins of his father and forefathers. He had even encouraged those servants of God who had returned to Jerusalem to also pray and fast the same way! What a conviction God had released upon them, and today we call this conviction "godly sorrow"!

Let's stop and think about our situation. If we are Christians and have not repented of living away from God and His Kingdom and we haven't thought about the first four chapters of this book, when are we going to wake up and repent? God can't use us until we see the demand that God has presented to us and then we humbly agree that we must repent fully and move forward with God! Restoration of God's Church will be a difficult job, with a lot of attacks from the enemy, but we can press through to victory!

Disobedience of God's people led to the complete destruction of Jerusalem and the temple. Over and over, God had told them to obey His commands, and if they violated them, to repent in sackcloth and ashes. We don't understand the meaning of that kind of repentance, but God is still holding us responsible for the ruins of His Church.

We need to seize the hurt that God feels and repent and weep in anguish, in brokenness, and shame that we have not followed God the way He has told us to follow. When Jesus said, "Pick up your cross and follow me," this was not a line to put in scripture so God's people could ignore it. It was a passionate plea from Jesus that was testifying the heart of God! Do you feel any remorse, guilt, pain, or grief in any way over the condition of your heart? Do you want to repent and work with God's restoration but you do not want to give up all of your worldly ways that are offensive to God?

Superficial praying will not get the job done! Through prayer and fasting and weeping, we must ask God to help us dig out the roots of our sin. We must listen to the Holy Spirit and even destroy the bloodline curses that have come down upon us from previous generations. Remember, the battle against our sin is dealing with the demonic, and God has the power for our victory. Revival only comes when we are right with God in every way!

> *If My people who are called by My name will humble themselves, and pray and seek My face, and turn from their wicked ways, then I will hear from heaven, and will forgive their sin and heal their land.* (2 Chronicles 7:14)

Repentance! We keep hearing that word over and over. God has opened a pathway for us to repent, and when we do and when we change, He can begin a work of restoration and revival in His Church. Then we can individually assess the condition of God's Church and plan and carry out His purpose of restoration.

> *Then I said to them, "You see the distress that we are in, how Jerusalem lies waste, and its gates are burned with fire. Come and let us build the wall of Jerusalem, that we may no longer be a reproach." And I told them of the hand of my God which had*

been good upon me, and of the king's words that he had spoken to me. So, they said, "Let us rise up and build." Then they set their hands to this good work.
(Nehemiah 2:17–18)

Two words issued a question and a challenge to each one of the fifty thousand workers. Do you see the distress we are in as churches around the world and that we are a reproach to God? This Hebrew word *cherpaah* is translated as *"reproach,"* and it means to be in shame or to disgrace.

So here we stand, hopefully with a pure heart, a sound mind, and being obedient to whatever God wants us to do in this work of restoration. We are ready, and now we must do what God shows us to do. I believe our most powerful tools of restoration are going to be the word of God and moving in His power! Our platform to work from will be "unity or being in one accord," learning how to be aggressive in our battles, and working in love with one another.

We must be in one accord and in unity with the Spirit. Our next obstacle will be the enemy. Don't be deceived in thinking that the enemy doesn't care if we rebuild and restore God's Church. He is going to revolt against us, but he will not prosper. We have been redeemed, cleansed by the blood of the Lamb, and we rule and reign in the heavenlies with Christ Jesus. Even when we continue to pray each day, we need to be aware that the enemy is plotting to stop our work of restoration.

But it so happened, when Sanballat heard that we were rebuilding the wall, that he was furious and very indignant, and mocked the Jews. And he spoke before his brethren and the army of Samaria, and said, "What are these feeble Jews doing? Will they fortify themselves? Will they offer sacrifices? Will they complete it in a day? Will they revive the stones from the heaps of rubbish, stones that are burned?"
Now Tobiah the Ammonite was beside him, and he said, "Whatever they build, if even a fox goes

up on it, he will break down their stone wall." Hear, O our God, for we are despised; turn their reproach on their own heads and give them as plunder to a land of captivity! Do not cover their iniquity, and do not let their sin be blotted out from before You; for they have provoked You to anger before the builders. So, we built the wall, and the entire wall was joined together up to half its height, for the people had a mind to work. (Nehemiah 4:1–6)

Opposition will come from the outside and even come from within the churches. Outside attempts to stop you will come from people who will say that what you are doing is not from God. They will tell you that it is impossible to rebuild a church that you cannot see with your physical eyes. Negative talk will come from people that you know and respect, even Christian brothers and sisters. Some may curse and call you names, ridicule you, and declare that you are insane! Just know that when the enemy gets stirred up, you are doing something that God has called you to do, and God supports you with His power.

Deception will come along. The works of deception can fool and confuse even the very elect. Temptation will arise and try to convince you that you are wrong, but God will forgive you anyway. They did the same thing to Nehemiah and the workers.

Now it happened, when Sanballat, Tobiah, the Arabs, the Ammonites, and the Ashdodites heard that the walls of Jerusalem were being restored and the gaps were beginning to be closed, that they became very angry, and all of them conspired together to come and attack Jerusalem and create confusion. Nevertheless, we made our prayer to our God, and because of them we set a watch against them day and night. (Nehemiah 4:7–9)

Here, we have enemies that are against one another, and now, they join forces to come and do battle with the workers on the walls.

It is so strange how hatred, anger, and bitterness can cause people to unify and attempt to destroy their common enemy. We see that happening right now in the United States of America's political systems. Leaders hating leaders with a fire and enough anger to destroy these enemies. But the solution to these threats is still prayer. They prayed to God and went about their work. They set up watches day and night to be alerted to the plans of the enemy attacks.

Jesus was involved in this same situation with the enemies who hated Him and wanted to kill Him. They went to great lengths to accomplish their devilish plans but failed to succeed. We even see in Scripture that there were important leaders who joined forces against Jesus.

> *Then Herod, with his men of war, treated Him with contempt and mocked Him, arrayed Him in a gorgeous robe, and sent Him back to Pilate. That very day Pilate and Herod became friends with each other, for previously they had been at enmity with each other.* (Luke 23:11–12)

The enemy brought the attack to Nehemiah, to Jesus, and they will bring it to you as well. Satan is out to destroy God's Church, and that includes us, but he will not prevail. Now, that is the frontal attack that we can see. Nehemiah also warned us about an attack covered in deception.

> *Now it happened when Sanballat, Tobiah, Geshem the Arab, and the rest of our enemies heard that I had rebuilt the wall, and that there were no breaks left in it (though at that time I had not hung the doors in the gates), that Sanballat and Geshem sent to me, saying, "Come, let us meet together among the villages in the plain of Ono." But they thought to do me harm.* (Nehemiah 6:1–2)

These demonic destroyers will not leave one stone in place until they try every form of destruction. The devil does not play games like many Christians do in our current season. He is focused on destruction, and no matter what it takes, he will continue his attacks. Like Jesus said:

> *Beware of false prophets, who come to you in sheep's clothing, but inwardly they are ravenous wolves. You will know them by their fruits. Do men gather grapes from thornbushes or figs from thistles? Even so, every good tree bears good fruit, but a bad tree bears bad fruit. A good tree cannot bear bad fruit, nor can a bad tree bear good fruit. Every tree that does not bear good fruit is cut down and thrown into the fire. Therefore, by their fruits you will know them.* (Matthew 7:15–20)

The enemy will also use lies and devious deceptions to turn your heart away from your labor and purpose. Again, Jesus warned us against this as well.

> *For false christs and false prophets will rise and show signs and wonders to deceive, if possible, even the elect. But take heed; see, I have told you all things beforehand.* (Mark 13:22–23)

Nehemiah knew the three enemies by name and reputation as well as the others that followed them. He knew that they were very deceptive and how to unveil their deceit. It is so important and necessary that we know who our enemies are, how to recognize them, and how to pray them down and destroy them. It's also important that we listen to God and do exactly what He says. God's Church will be raised up in a glorious victory! Praise God!

Chapter 6

Unity and Offensive Positions

Working in unity is the only way we can be successful in the Kingdom of God. Nehemiah and the men had been working diligently. Did they have any problems? Absolutely! God had given them wisdom and determination to complete the rebuilding. After they had built the wall up halfway, another problem surfaced.

> *Then Sanballat sent his servant to me as before, the fifth time, with an open letter in his hand. In it was written: It is reported among the nations, and Geshem says, that you and the Jews plan to rebel; therefore, according to these rumors, you are rebuilding the wall, that you may be their king. And you have also appointed prophets to proclaim concerning you at Jerusalem, saying, "There is a king in Judah!" Now these matters will be reported to the king. So come, therefore, and let us consult together.*
>
> *Then I sent to him, saying, "No such things as you say are being done, but you invent them in your own heart." For they all were trying to make us afraid, saying, "Their hands will be weakened in the work, and it will not be done." Now therefore, O God, strengthen my hands. (Nehemiah 6:5–9)*

The enemy was all around them with physical and verbal attacks. Resistance was the enemy's plot to confuse them and halt the work on the walls. So did this stop the work? Were they overcome with fear and quit building? Did they cry out to Nehemiah to stop the building and abandon the work that God had called them to do? *No!* They kept right on working. So what did Nehemiah do about these threats? He continued to build the wall! Oh, he put in place some other displays of protection, but the work of watching and building continued.

Listen, this was God's plan, and nothing in heaven or on the earth could stop His plan from being finished unless the workers gave up. That's a lesson for us today. We have been called as Christians to rebuild God's Church. God will be in control, and He has a plan. The first step is that you and I repent and get right with God, heal our differences with one another, and be about our Heavenly Father's business. We will just keep working and handle every threat of the enemy by trusting our Lord. God is much greater in battling the enemy than we could ever be. Our responsibility is to have in our hearts a mind to work. Our fighting is done in our prayers!

Now, I want to point out what can be a major problem that will not only stop the work but will discourage the workers. Nehemiah identified this problem in the next verse.

> *Then Judah said, "The strength of the laborers*
> *is failing, and there is so much rubbish that we are*
> *not able to build the wall.* (Nehemiah 4:10)

They had learned how to handle the attacks that came from the outside, but now, internal problems were rising. The workers are worn out because there was too much rubble and ruins left, and they could not continue to build the wall. Something needed to be done to resolve the discouragement.

The answer was to remove the rubbish! You can't build a strong wall or install gates when the rubbish is too high and unstable. We call this using common sense. The foundation under the walls is critical to the stability and the length of time the walls will stand.

> *For they all were trying to make us afraid, saying, "Their hands will be weakened in the work, and it will not be done." Now therefore, O God, strengthen my hands.* (Nehemiah 6:9)

They prayed: "O God, strengthen my hands." I believe Nehemiah had a word from God to split up the workforce. This would alleviate the weakness from laboring long hours, and the men would swap off and get the job done.

> *So it was, from that time on, that half of my servants worked at construction, while the other half held the spears, the shields, the bows, and wore armor; and the leaders were behind all the house of Judah. Those who built on the wall, and those who carried burdens, loaded themselves so that with one hand they worked at construction, and with the other held a weapon. Every one of the builders had his sword girded at his side as he built. And the one who sounded the trumpet was beside me.* (Nehemiah 4:16–18)

> *And I also say to you that you are Peter, and on this rock, I will build My church, and the gates of Hades shall not prevail against it. And I will give you the keys of the kingdom of heaven, and whatever you bind on earth will be bound in heaven, and whatever you loose on earth will be loosed in heaven.* (Matthew 16:18–19)

There is a vital lesson to be learned in this encounter of too much rubbish. Every one of us have rubbish in our lives, and we are trying to be a part of a move of God in rebuilding God's Church.

We can't build anything on rubble and rubbish. So we need to clean everything out of the way in our personal lives and begin our rebuilding on solid ground.

We need to be "in Christ Jesus" to help cleanse the church. The first part of this book is built on recognizing our sin (our rubbish and ruins) and dealing with them through prayer and repentance and godly sorrow. Remember, this is God's house we are going to rebuild, and it is absolutely necessary that we be clean, holy, and walking with Christ Jesus in the way He has taught us.

Jesus describes the foundation upon which He would build His church, and now, we can have the honor of helping to restore that church. You and Jesus working together. Let's restore the Church on the rock!

I want to highlight the attacks of the enemy against Nehemiah and the workers to enable us to be prepared for the intense and huge job that lies ahead. God has the plan, and we have the desire to rebuild and the confidence in knowing that God's Church must be "without spot or wrinkle."

This had been an exciting time for Nehemiah as we see the declaration recorded in the following statement: "So, the wall was finished on the twenty-fifth day of Elul, in fifty-two days" (Nehemiah 6:15).

That had to be a God thing. The wall was two and a half miles long, forty feet tall, and eight feet thick. Quite an accomplishment in such a short time! But we are looking back at the victory that Nehemiah and the people of Jerusalem attained. However, we are looking forward to the work and the battles that will occur as we move toward rebuilding God's Church. Remember, the devil is violently opposed to the moving of God's Spirit in revival and awakening.

He will attempt to delay or stop the rebuilding of God's Church and quench the fires of revival! God hears us say, "Let us arise and build," and satan says, "Let us arise and stop them." Remember, we are rebuilding not only God's Church, but we are also rebuilding the spiritual walls around our personal lives!

Now, let's refresh our minds as to how the enemy will work to stop our rebuilding. His first devious plan is to attempt to manipulate our minds.

> *Now it happened when Sanballat, Tobiah, Geshem the Arab, and the rest of our enemies heard that I had rebuilt the wall, and that there were no breaks left in it (though at that time I had not hung the doors in the gates), that Sanballat and Geshem sent to me, saying, "Come, let us meet together among the villages in the plain of Ono." But they thought to do me harm. So, I sent messengers to them, saying, "I am doing a great work, so that I cannot come down. Why should the work cease while I leave it and go down to you?"* (Nehemiah 6:1–3)

In these verses, we see Nehemiah working hard to rebuild the broken walls. The enemy, however, is calling Nehemiah to "come down to the plain, and we will meet together." Come down to our level. Don't be so fanatical and extreme. You are too narrow-minded. Come on down, and let's reason this thing out.

What we need to see in this example is that the devil is always trying to manipulate our minds by telling us that we need to compromise! He wants us to live by reason and not by faith and trusting God! The devil wants us to compromise because everyone else is doing it; at least that's what he wants us to believe. Satan is primarily concerned with manipulating our minds to the point that he will lead us to compromise. So how did Nehemiah reply to this demonic offer?

> *I am doing a great work and I cannot come down. Why should the work stop while I leave it and come down to you?* (Nehemiah 6:3)

Do you see or hear any compromise in Nehemiah's reply? A greater question would be: "What will you do?" The devil is already planning on how to drag you down! He is already out to get you to compromise! He will make statements like, "Has God really said" that you need to really be a part of this rebuilding? It's okay. You can fudge a little bit on your commitment. Live with me in sin; no one will ever know, and you can pretend to build the building!

Or your reply to satan's invitation to shirk your duties and responsibility must be, "I am doing a great work for God, and I cannot come down and follow you! I see your devilish plot and subtle tactics, and I will not be a part! You will not manipulate my mind!"

I can hear people now. You shared some of this earlier, so why are you repeating what has already been said? The answer is that we learn quicker through repetition. Listen, working in restoring God's Church is not going to be an easy task. We are going to have to stay alert, know what the plan is, and not be sidetracked by anyone or any demonic power!

The next thing is that satan will try is to alter your reason for building.

> *Then Sanballat sent his servant to me as before, the fifth time, with an open letter in his hand. In it was written: It is reported among the nations, and Geshem says, that you and the Jews plan to rebel; therefore, according to these rumors, you are rebuilding the wall, that you may be their king.*
>
> *And you have also appointed prophets to proclaim concerning you at Jerusalem, saying, "There is a king in Judah!" Now these matters will be reported to the king. So come, therefore, and let us consult together.* (Nehemiah 6:5–7)

If the devil cannot get us to compromise, he will spread rumors about us and try to produce doubt about our motives! An example of this would be a Christian that is all out for saving souls and a heart for God. He/she will probably become a victim of gossip. He/she may be called a "Jesus freak!" The devil will see to that! If we really become sold out to the glory of God and Jesus, we shouldn't be surprised when the devil fabricates lies about us!

Now, what was Nehemiah's reaction to this second attempt to stop the work?

> *Then I sent to him, saying, "No such things as you say are being done, but you invent them in your own heart." For they all were trying to make us afraid, saying, "Their hands will be weakened in the work, and it will not be done." Now therefore, O God, strengthen my hands.* (Nehemiah 6:8–9)

Those lies did not divert Nehemiah one inch. Satan's attempt to get Nehemiah upset by altering his motives failed miserably!

Listen, Nehemiah was not concerned in what others thought about him. He had one consuming passion in life, and that was to rebuild those broken walls! What about us? Do you have a passion in your spirit to get God's Church up and going, to make an impact in the United States, and to see revival break out all over the world?

Do you think satan will celebrate with you in your newfound motives and heartfelt desires to obey God? Before any of you get all proud and puffed up, be sure and test the spirits around you! You must be aware of satan's plans and purpose, so you can destroy them! Open your eyes to the devil's subtle points. He will try to manipulate your mind; he will try to misrepresent your reason for building; and if both of these fail, he will try to activate the third thing you need to remember—to change or alter your mission.

> *Afterward I came to the house of Shemaiah the son of Delaiah, the son of Mehetabel, who was a secret informer; and he said, "Let us meet together in the house of God, within the temple, and let us close the doors of the temple, for they are coming to kill you; indeed, at night they will come to kill you."* (Nehemiah 6:10)

Here, we have a man posing as a prophet, and he was urging Nehemiah to flee to the temple and stay there, lest the enemy should slay him! Same perverted plan used today by the enemy!

The Apostle John warned us of the same plan that would be used by the enemy!

> *Beloved, do not believe every spirit, but test the spirits, whether they are of God, because many false prophets have gone out into the world. By this you know the Spirit of God: Every spirit that confesses that Jesus Christ has come in the flesh is of God, and every spirit that does not confess that Jesus Christ has come in the flesh is not of God. And this is the spirit of the Antichrist, which you have heard was coming, and is now already in the world.* (1 John 4:1–3)

Our responsibility is to be aware of false prophets in our present day and to know that they are trying to mislead us and destroy our mission!

Satan was attempting to change Nehemiah's mission. He was trying to induce Nehemiah into shirking his responsibilities. He was attempting to attract him with a cheap religion that would not compel him to carry a cross! The enemy will try to do the same thing with us! He will try to involve us in "good" things, but things without the power of the Holy Spirit and the message of salvation. If you don't believe that, all you have to do is look around at other churches today.

The devil has changed the pastor's mission. They once reached out with the message of salvation, and today, they have changed their mission and are struggling to make their budgets and watching their memberships decline with every passing year! Do you see that happening to other churches. How about your church?

So what was Nehemiah's reaction to this third plot to halt revival?

> *And I said, "Should such a man as I flee? And who is there such as I who would go into the temple to save his life? I will not go in!* (Nehemiah 6:11)

Nehemiah was committed to his mission—the rebuilding of those broken walls. Nothing, not even the devil, could alter or stop the building of Nehemiah's mission!

When you get started, how will you handle satan when he comes to change your individual mission? Satan's fourth and final attempt to stop you is that he will "deceive you."

> *Also, in those days the nobles of Judah sent many letters to Tobiah, and the letters of Tobiah came to them. For many in Judah were pledged to him, because he was the son-in-law of Shechaniah the son of Arah, and his son Jehohanan had married the daughter of Meshullam the son of Berechiah. Also, they reported his good deeds before me, and reported my words to him. Tobiah sent letters to frighten me. (Nehemiah 6:17–19)*

This passage of scripture shows us just how easily the devil can deceive! Judah was conspiring with the enemy! Think about it! Judah, of all people, a part of the lineage of Jesus, was working with the enemy to stop the rebuilding and destroy Nehemiah!

Today, satan will try to do the same thing! Satan will try to divert real revival by misguiding the reality of what God is showing us. It is dangerous to follow anyone in the Christian life apart from the Lord Jesus. We are to follow Jesus! He is our example! So let me warn you! Keep your eyes on Jesus and no one else! Let's get started rebuilding God's Church, and together, we will keep an eye on satan to make sure he does not stop what we have set out to do!

Chapter 7

Reviewing Principles
of Rebuilding

I can't emphasize enough the importance of what we are about to do. Our project or job looks impossible, and right now, we need to think about what we are going to do. Jesus was dealing with a father who had a son who was demon-possessed. The father asked Jesus for help, and the answer Jesus gave this father is the same answer He is giving us right now.

Jesus said to him, "If you can believe, all things
are possible to him who believes." (Mark 9:23)

Like Nehemiah, we must see beyond the impossibilities and focus on the possible! No turning back, no shrinking in fear, no room for doubt, and we must join together in unity. We must believe this is possible because God has called us to the task.

So let's move on in rebuilding God's Church. We need to rebuild churches that man has built, and our personal lives at the same time. Now, there are seven levels of change that we need to incorporate into our personal lives and walk in them daily. They are the following:

1. Repentance and reconciliation

2. Love
3. Respect for the Scriptures
4. Reverence for Jesus
5. Confession of our sin
6. Pursuing joy in our service
7. Renewing our commitment to God

Nehemiah, the man of God, had rebuilt the wall around Jerusalem that had been torn down and the gates that had been burned with fire! His physical wall was finished!

> *So the wall was finished on the twenty-fifth day of Elul, in fifty-two days. And it happened, when all our enemies heard of it, and all the nations around us saw these things, that they were very disheartened in their own eyes; for they perceived that this work was done by our God.* (Nehemiah 6:15–16)

Jerusalem was rebuilt in fifty-two days! Even with fifty thousand committed workers, it still seemed impossible. But it was not! Our spiritual wall of God's Church and our personal life is just starting! As Nehemiah finished the job, we can learn principles of rebuilding. The greatest and first principle is getting in a tight, personal relationship with God and knowing you can do what God requires.

We don't have physical walls with wood and stones to rebuild, but we do have spiritual walls that need to be rebuilt in God's Church and in all our personal lives. The core group of this rebuilding task has heard enough of the principles of rebuilding to get started. In learning from Nehemiah, we have been dealing with circumstances and conditions which bring about revival. Nehemiah had said: "The walls were completed." Revival had come.

Now, we've learned how to bring revival. What happens when the walls are completed in God's Church? There are certain things that will happen to indicate that we are serious about rebuilding God's Church, and we are hungry for revival.

> *Now all the people gathered together as one man in the open square that was in front of the water gate; and they told Ezra the scribe to bring the book of the law of Moses, which the LORD had commanded Israel.* (Nehemiah 8:1)

Notice that in this verse, it says that *"all the people were in unity in the family of God."* There was reconciliation within the family of God.

The first thing we must obtain is repentance and reconciliation. These two words are the beginning place with God in giving your life to Jesus. God designed a plan where Jesus, the Son of God, would lay down His life in atonement for the sin of the world. When we identified Jesus as God's Son and realized that Jesus died, was buried, and was raised from the dead, then we have an open door to invite Jesus into our life. This new life comes through repentance. We confess to God that our lives are full of sin, and we ask Him to forgive us. We then ask Jesus to come into our lives, and we become new creations in Christ Jesus. God calls this act "salvation!"

The second thing we need to remember is that before and during the rebuilding of the walls, all the Israelites were not in unity! Right now, in churches in our nation and even around the world, there is a similar problem that needs repentance and reconciliation. We need to come together as a family and give ourselves to loving one another!

> *Jesus said to him, "You shall love the Lord your God with all your heart, with all your soul, and with all your mind. This is the first and great commandment. And the second is like it: You shall love your neighbor as yourself."* (Matthew 22:37)

We are going to need an outreach of love. Love is a fruit of the Spirit and of revival, but we must also learn to live in love with each other; we need to release this love in churches everywhere! People are hungry for love; they need to be needed, they are hurting, and they need someone to show them that we care! This is true with the people of the world and even in the lives of a lot of Christians.

I said this is a fruit of revival, and it is. However, we were called to this kind of love by Jesus, and we should already be operating in this love! Love is also a fruit of unity.

> *Can two walk together, unless they are agreed?*
> (Amos 3:3)

Also, the words of Jesus:

> *And if a house is divided against itself, that house cannot stand.* (Mark 3:25)

This divisive spirit is a dangerous part of the Jezebel spirit. We need to learn how to recognize this spirit and cast it out of its habitation, whether it is in your life or in man's churches or if it is found as a part of the ruins in God's Church!

If Jesus came into your church, how would He recognize the brethren?

> *By this all will know that you are My disciples, if you have love for one another.* (John 13:35)

Love is the only thing that can bring true unity and reconciliation. If we are going to work together in unity and harmony, each one of us must have the "agape love" that Jesus is talking about! How can we ever get anywhere if any of us are holding a grudge against someone or harboring resentment against someone or not reconciled with someone in your heart?

When the people of God are in unity and harmony, they can function as "one person." When we are in unity, we can hold to one hope, one goal, and move the same way. Do you see that?

> *Now all the people gathered together as one man in the open square that was in front of the water gate; and they told Ezra the scribe to bring the book of the law of Moses, which the LORD had commanded Israel.*
>
> *So Ezra the priest brought the law before the assembly of men and women and all who could hear with understanding on the first day of the seventh month.*
>
> *Then he read from it in the open square that was in front of the water gate from morning until midday, before the men and women and those who could understand; and the ears of all the people were attentive to the book of the law.* (Nehemiah 8:1–3)

Our third responsibility as born-again children of God is that we must be developing a love and respect for the scriptures. That's what happened with the people in Nehemiah's day. Their experience in rebuilding the wall changed their heart, and they began to pursue the reading and hearing the Word of God "daily!" You and I need to read and focus our thoughts in the Word of God daily so we can continue to be filled with the Spirit of God and the wisdom and purity of God! The Word of God is a major part of bringing revival.

Perhaps you might admit that you do not read the Bible like you should or you do not spend time in God's Word daily. It is not a part of your daily routine and life. Then I respectfully declare that you need to repent of your neglect! God's Word is a major part of bringing revival! All of us need to commit to reading and meditating on God's Word daily!

Now, we are not rebuilding physical things. We are rebuilding our personal Christian lives, and the *hope* (emphasis mine) of God's Church is to be received by the Bridegroom, Jesus, "without spot or wrinkle."

The fourth thing we are going to need in this restored church is reverence for Jesus!

> *And Ezra blessed the LORD, the great God. Then all the people answered, "Amen, Amen!" while lifting up their hands. And they bowed their heads and worshipped the Lord with their faces to the ground.* (Nehemiah 8:6)

The people began to bless the Lord and praise Him! They lifted their hands in reverence to their God! They bowed low in prayer and worshipped the Lord! Part of our life change will be to learn to bless and worship the Lord on a regular basis, especially from our heart. Have you ever thought about how we love God to bless us with His love? How about you personally? Do you worship God each day?

The most appropriate way to approach God in prayer is through praise! The psalmist exhorted:

> *Enter into His gates with thanksgiving, and into His courts with praise. Be thankful to Him and bless His name. For the Lord is good; His mercy is everlasting, and His truth endures to all generations.* (Psalm 100:4–5)

If you do not spend any time in praise and worship, you should repent of your neglect, confess it as sin, and ask the Spirit of God to help change your life!

A fifth thing that we need to identify is the confession of our sin! We have talked about repentance earlier, which is most important, but now, we must renounce or do away with all sin and not return to this destructive work in our lives. This kind of praying will lead to godly sorrow.

> *And Nehemiah, who was the governor, Ezra the priest and scribe, and the Levites who taught the people said to all the people, "This day is holy to the Lord your God; do not mourn nor weep." For all the people wept when they heard the words of the law.* (Nehemiah 8:9)

This is one area that is completely foreign to the American church and even in many churches around the world. We do not walk in brokenness over our sin! Most Christians today do not weep over their sin or over their knowledge of the lost people around them! If Nehemiah's people could be convicted, if they could weep over their rebellion, then they should confess the hurt and brokenness because they had ignored God's law. What about us? The word that we are supposed to live by is Jesus and the written Word!

> *In the beginning was the Word, and the Word was with God, and the Word was God."* (John 1:1)

> *And the Word became flesh and dwelt among us, and we beheld His glory, the glory as of the only begotten of the Father, full of grace and truth.* (John 1:14)

Yet the closer we come to the heart of God, the more we realize that we are like filthy rags in His sight! When we walk in renunciation of our sins, the more we come to acknowledge our condition. The more we see our condition as God sees it, the closer we want to press into God! Do you see how important our righteousness and purity will be when we begin the labor of rebuilding?

So how does God see our sin? Let's see just how clear God's message to us is about sin.

> *If we say that we have no sin, we deceive ourselves, and the truth is not in us.*
> *If we confess our sins, He is faithful and just to forgive us our sins and to cleanse us from all unrighteousness.*
> *If we say that we have not sinned, we make Him a liar, and His word is not in us.* (1 John 1:8–10)

The sixth thing we need to identify is pursuing joy in our service.

> *For this day is holy to our Lord. Do not sorrow,*
> *for the joy of the Lord is your strength.* (Nehemiah
> 8:10b)

Do you know what real joy is? It is in the service of Jesus and, particularly, in leading others to know Him! The joy of the Lord is dependent upon obedience to God! Jesus only did what He saw His Father doing. Let's do that for a season and see how quickly the atmosphere in our churches will change.

Even Jesus was totally obedient, even unto death!

> *Looking unto Jesus, the author and finisher of*
> *our faith, who for the joy that was set before Him*
> *endured the cross, despising the shame, and has*
> *sat down at the right hand of the throne of God.*
> (Hebrews 12:2b)

Jesus found His greatest joy in doing the will of His Father!

Are you convinced now that it's God's will for us to rebuild His Church? Do you think it's God's will for us to reach out to the lost in love? All of us have a divine purpose! It's time to get started and not look back!

The seventh thing we need to pursue is to renew our commitment to God and His Kingdom. How long has it been since you renewed your commitment that you made to God and His Church? A commitment is not just attending a church. A commitment to God is a promise to serve God, carry out your calling, find your place of service, and serve faithfully. Don't slip away from His presence again! Declare the Gospel wherever you are, lay hands on the sick, cast out demons, and serve in the fields that are white unto harvest.

Let us rise up and build! We will never have joy and will never be happy outside the will of God for our lives! Let's choose to obey God and rejoice in the work He has laid before us! "The joy of the Lord is our strength!"

Chapter 8

Rebuilding Through Love

As we move forward, we've got to have the Holy Spirit inside us, empowering us and leading us with each step we take—a Spirit of boldness filling our soul! We cannot do this by ourselves living in fleshly bodies. Jesus depended on God the Father and the Holy Spirit to enable Him to work in power while He was on this earth. We must do the same!

We must work and live out of the love that Jesus had in His commitment to His Father. *Love!* The "agape" love that God the Father has poured into our lives.

> *Jesus said to him, "You shall love the Lord your God with all your heart, with all your soul, and with all your mind. This is the first and great commandment. And the second is like it: 'You shall love your neighbor as yourself. On these two commandments hang all the Law and the Prophets."* (Matthew 22:37–39)

This love is not situational, and it's not an impossible emotion that we cannot attain! It is an absolute in our lives as we live and work in the Kingdom of God! Without love, our task of rebuilding our lives and God's Church will be literally impossible! We are going to glorify our God by being obedient and by pouring out His love through each one of our lives!

So out of love, let's promise to serve God, carry His calling on our life, find our place of service and serve faithfully, and not slip away from His presence! A commitment to God is to declare the Gospel wherever you are! Will you do that?

The greatest revelation to the church in this next season is going to be love. Without love, we are nothing, and what we accomplish profits nothing without it! It does not make any difference how many of the giftings you can operate in! If you do not have love and compassion in your heart, then you produce nothing of lasting value! Love is to be our greatest destiny. Paul wrote to the Corinthian Church:

Though I speak with the tongues of men and of angels, but have not love, I have become sounding brass or a clanging cymbal. (1 Corinthians 13:1)

Love is going to be established in the Church of Jesus Christ! It will be perfected in the church. Everything that is not of love and true faith will be shaken. Love will open hearts and doors of many nations. Let's purpose in our hearts to grow in love.

If we don't know how to rebuild and restore in love, God is going to cross your path with people you know and have no compassion for! You will be confronted with your lack of love and compassion for these people that have caused you grief, anger, and despair. You may have rejected these people for years because of the expectations you put on them that they were not able to live up to!

So get ready to deal with each individual situation! These confrontations will not be about changing them, but they will be about God exposing your heart! God wants you to change! God wants your heart to be filled with His love!

There will also be manifestations of angels in times ahead, but not in the realm we are looking for. They will come to you as the unwanted, the unlovely, the unaccepted, and the unlovable. You will not discern that you are entertaining angels! Your heart will be measured by the love and compassion that you extend to them in ministry. We will no longer be able to measure ourselves by ourselves. We will not be measured by our abilities, but by the measure of love that is found in our hearts! Truly, our motivations will be tested and shaken in the years to come as God measures our capacity to love!

There is a fresh anointing of love that is here for those who hunger. This love will consume the heart and will even become a double anointing as it is given away; it begins right now! Love can no longer be ignored or presumed. Love is God! His heart will open to those who hunger and thirst for that love!

Love is a revelation of the new season to come. So what do we do about it? There are several things that we can set in place in our lives that will cause us to mature and walk in the revelations of our past years. They are perhaps broad in nature, but they are certainly able to accomplish what God intends.

First, ask the Holy Spirit to bring again the revelations that you have seen in the last few years. These revelations will now be the pathway for the next years to come. Write them down and focus your thoughts on them. Ask the Lord to manifest them in this next season of your life.

Second, ask the Holy Spirit to convict you of any area of your life where you have not submitted to Him. Ask Him to cleanse you of every sin and every evil, wicked way. Ask the Holy Spirit to destroy every enemy that is against the love that abides in your heart. Ask Him to fill you with God's love. Above all, complete submission to the Lord in this next season is absolutely necessary!

Third, ask the Lord to increase His grace upon your life as you seek after Him. Take time to fast and pray every day. There is going to be warfare over this next season, but you can establish the victory right now. Hide yourself in His grace. Grace is the key to victory!

Fourth, ask the Lord to quicken personal promises to you from His Word. Stand on those promises. Write them down. Rehearse these things. Remember, God's Word does not return to Him void. It will accomplish everything God has sent His Word to do!

Fifth, praise Him! Praise Him and establish Him in the highest place in your life. Remind yourself of His worthiness and greatness! Praise is always an instrument of victory in every battle!

Sixth, pray and praise in tongues. Welcome His mysteries to be revealed in your spirit through the gift of tongues. Hunger for the mysteries of God. There are so many things that God is going to reveal. Make sure you are tuned in to heaven with a listening ear!

Seventh, invite the Lord to give you strategies for every area of your life for this present season. Get ready to build or move into what He is showing you. Some of you are going to receive strategies for new employment or new business ventures. Some will receive strategies for building wealth for the Kingdom of God. Some will receive strategies for building new relationships that will cause you to prosper! So ask for and receive new strategies that God has already prepared for you in this season. God wants you to prosper in the midst of rebuilding His Church!

Eighth, ask the Holy Spirit to fill you afresh with His presence that you might go forth in the fullness of His will, His purpose, and His power. There is a worship song titled "You Are Welcome, Holy Spirit." It was written by Evangelist Jimmy Swaggart of Baton Rouge, Louisiana. Accept and receive the Holy Spirit's presence and His power! Allow Him to take complete control of your life! Acknowledge Him as your Comforter and Counselor. Identify Him as the Living Water and the Ever-flowing Fountain. Submit to His leadership and control.

Hear the Holy Spirit in this hour as He calls you to go into the fields that are white unto harvest as a worker. You will go into these fields with power and might. You will be a demonstration of God's Kingdom as love captures and draws people into the Kingdom of God! The time is short. There is no more time to delay! Hear what the Spirit of God is saying in this hour and respond with your whole heart! Amen?

Jesus is the Head of the Body of Christ, the Church. We are His body! He is looking forward one day to return to earth to receive His Bride, which is you and me, and He expects His bride to be clean, "without spot or wrinkle."

Chapter 9

Reality Time

We are involved in another terrorist attack on the church and this nation! This attack is not physical; it is spiritual! An army of demonic forces has been loosed on this nation to destroy her! An army of hatred, bitterness, fear, anger, insanity, delusion, and even attempts to destroy our nation from the inside out. Leaders in Washington have become delusional! Some leaders in Washington, DC, are making futile attempts to take over the power of our nation! Even our churches are under attack by extremists. We find that one of the major demonic weapons is lying!

Yes, we saw our nation rally eighteen years ago after 9/11; our president rallied, and even some of the elected leaders in Washington rallied for the cause of freedom! That was good! Patriotism was restored in America for a season. Prayer had been restored in the lives of many Americans during that terrible time! That was urgently needed!

But patriotism and prayer are not the complete answer to what faces this nation! It's a start! But not the complete answer!

Our nation has responded and churches responded with compassion for those who were hurting and abandoned. But we've yet to see anything mentioned or any compassion expressed for those who are lost and are going to hell! Hearts have still not turned to the gospel of Jesus Christ! So many people in this nation think that heaven and eternal life are theirs just because they live in America! We are a deceived nation!

Sin is the root of our problem, and satan is the destroyer! Our personal sin and our national sin have opened the doors to destruction, and we should not be moved by what the critics say! We are going to have to repent of the sins of this nation! If we refuse to repent or if we remain passive about our sin and our relationship with God as a nation, then we are going to keep the door to destruction wide open!

This nation needs God more than any other time in history! There is a deep darkness overtaking our world right now, even in our nation. But God is still in control! He is still seated on His throne in heaven. God still loves America, and it's only by His Grace that you and I are here today anyway.

But we must see that without a strong message of repentance and a strong response to repentance, we are still in trouble. It is time for the church to stand up and be the *example* for this nation! This is a part of rebuilding God's Church!

The church has been meek, passive, and unrepentant long enough. The Lord has shared a verse of scripture many times for His Church, and I will share it again. This is the only reaction that God can respond to. I will share it out of the Message Bible, with contemporary language so we can all understand.

> *And if my people, my God-defined people, respond by humbling themselves, praying, seeking my presence, and turning their backs on their wicked lives, I'll be there ready for you: I'll listen from heaven, forgive their sins, and restore their land to health. From now on I'm alert day and night to the prayers offered at this place.* (2 Chronicles 7:14)

America has been called the melting pot of the nations. As a result, we have received people from all over this world as well as their religions and their sin. Their religion and sin have been mixed with our religion and sin. We are like the city of Athens, Greece, back during Paul's ministry. The whole city was corrupt with idols and religions from all over the world.

Today, in our nation alone, we have Hindus, Muslims, Hari Krishnas, Seventh Day Adventists, Mormons, Islamic, Buddhist, Catholics, Jews, as well as Protestant denominations, just to name a few. We have religions that are isolated by race. We have religions that are led by gays and lesbians. There are also demonic-based religions. If you can name it, you can find it in America.

This is the same thing that Paul saw in Athens. But just like in Paul's day, there are two things that God will not compromise: salvation and sin. Paul preached a message of salvation and repentance to the people of that city, just like we need to hear preached in this nation today.

God's Church must openly be demonstrated to the world around us with the gospel and the power. The church needs to preach the gospel. Christians need to preach the gospel also. That's part of the responsibility of every Christian—"to preach the gospel." Listen to Jesus:

> *And He said to them, "Go into all the world and preach the gospel to every creature. He who believes and is baptized will be saved; but he who does not believe will be condemned. And these signs will follow those who believe: In My name they will cast out demons; they will speak with new tongues; they will take up serpents; and if they drink anything deadly, it will by no means hurt them; they will lay hands on the sick, and they will recover."*
> (Mark 16:15–18)

Is that clear?

It's one thing to know about God and another thing to *know God!* Our nation, as well as many of our churches, know about God, but God is not satisfied with that.

> *You believe that there is one God; you do well!*
> *The devils or demons also believe, and they tremble!*
> (James 2:19)

Our failure as Christians and as Americans is that we do not *know God* intimately in a relationship. Therefore, that's why sin is so easy to cause us to fall. That's why our nation is full of sin, even to the point where God is being removed from everything that we believe in. Our relationship with God is controlled by religion, tradition, and deception! That's why we think everything is alright, but it is not.

During 9/11, at least 2,977 people died on that day. People are still dying today, eighteen years later, due to health problems caused by the dust and smoke. Cancer is one of those deadly diseases destroying survivors today. I wonder, How many of those actually had a relationship with Jesus and were ushered into His Presence?

How many Christians knew these people, but they never spoke to them about Jesus? How many died and went to hell because they thought sin was alright? Or they thought sin was not alright, but you always have plenty of time to deal with it later and seek after some religion. After all, sin abounds all around them, and God is a God of love, so why worry? We'll all make it to heaven in our own way, right?

No! That's the lie some in this nation believe. There is only one way to heaven. That is to "repent of your sins" and accept the free gift of God's Son Jesus. You take His life, and you lay down your life for Him. That's why the message of repentance is the key to our future. Repentance is the only weapon that we can use to bring our enemy down into the pits.

In times past, some have declared the world is going to end in ten years. *Big lie!* What they need to be declaring is that people are going to go to hell without Jesus. That is the *real truth!*

Paul said basically the same thing to the people in Athens, Greece.

> *And the times of this ignorance God ignored
> and allowed to pass unnoticed. But now, He com-
> mands all men to repent!* (Acts 17:30)

A city or a nation that has not heard the gospel of Jesus Christ has grace poured into it. But a city or a nation that has heard the gospel, *"God commands that they repent!"* Is that a clear statement? No options. No arguments. No waiting. He commands that they repent.

That's the message that is ringing clear and loud in my spirit, and I believe it is ringing in spirits all over America. Repent! But why?

> *Because God has appointed a day (or has fixed a day) when He will judge the world in righteousness by that man whom He has ordained (or appointed); God has given conviction, assurance and evidence by raising this same man from the dead!* (Acts 17:31)

Who is that man? His name is Jesus. Will God have a time of judgment? Absolutely! Is it already set on the calendar of God? Yes, it is. Can we change it, postpone it, or avoid it? Absolutely not!

If we do not think about it or if we are denying it, will not make it go away. It will happen just as sure as those planes of destruction had a day set in the hearts of those terrorists. Nothing could have stopped it. Nothing will delay the coming of God's judgment.

Does God still love us? Yes! He sent Jesus to die for us, and it was His will that nobody should perish without eternal hope in Christ. God still loves the sinner. God still loves this nation. But God does not love the sin. It is sin that destroys. Do you see that?

That's why God is calling "all men in our world unto repentance." Do you understand that? Does that include you and me? Yes, it does! How do I know what to repent of? Ask Him. He's not hiding it from you. You are the one hiding it from yourself. Unrepentant sin is what keeps you from having compassion for the lost that live all around you. Do you know what you were saved for? To be a witness for Jesus. Your sin has you deceived, and you are in hiding so that no one will find out. But wake up. *God knows!*

He knows your hidden sin. He knows that you are the key to salvation for those around you. But God has done all He can do. It's up to you right now.

We need to cry out:

God, help us to see how miserably we have failed You. God, help us to see how miserably we have failed those around us when we keep quiet about Jesus. God, help us to see how sin abounds in this nation and in many of our lives and what it is doing to our eternal salvation. God, help us to see that our eyes are blind.

Lift us up out of this pit of despair, and set our feet back on the Rock, Jesus Christ. God, set our souls on fire for Jesus. Fill our hearts with oil so that the fire never goes out. God, help us to set the example for this nation in this time of Your turning the heart of this nation back to You. Oh, God, forgive us of our sins! God, we repent for everything that is not right in our lives. Lord, we want to see revival fall on this nation! Right now, Lord. Right now!

Paul told the Athenians:

So that they should seek God, in the hope that they might feel (or grope) after Him and find Him! He is not far from each one of us. For in Him we live and move and have our being! (Acts 17:27–28a)

Pray for our nation!
Pray for God's Church and the churches across this nation!
Pray for each other!
Pray for yourself!
Pray for revival to impact this nation!
Pray that God's Church will be restored quickly!

Chapter 10

What Is the Plan to Rebuild?

For us to build anything, there must be a plan that gives us the details of the construction or the rebuilding of a structure. In the beginning of creation, God had a plan.

> *In the beginning God created the heavens and the earth. The earth was without form, and void; and darkness was on the face of the deep. And the Spirit of God was hovering over the face of the waters.* (Genesis 1:1–2)

When Adam and Eve fell out of grace in the Garden, God had to implement another plan.

> *Then the LORD God said, "Behold, the man has become like one of us, to know good and evil. And now, lest he put out his hand and take also of the tree of life, and eat, and live forever."*
> *Therefore the LORD God sent him out of the garden of Eden to till the ground from which he was taken.*
> *So He drove out the man; and He placed cherubim at the east of the garden of Eden, and a flam-*

ing sword which turned every way, to guard the way to the tree of life. (Genesis 3:22–24)

Throughout history, God dealt with His creation, working toward a new plan that would change the hearts of His people. He stepped out of the Old Covenant into a New Covenant when Jesus the Christ was born in Bethlehem. Jesus lived on this earth fully as a man (in the flesh) and fully as a Spirit, who would lay down His life on a cross and be sacrificed for the sin of the world. Through Christ Jesus, a new plan was offered to the world to be born again, to receive forgiveness of their sin, and to be raised to walk in newness of life by believing in Him. We call this salvation. God also sent His Holy Spirit to fill us and enable us to walk the Christian walk. This plan would show the world how much God loves His creation!

For God so loved the world that He gave His only begotten Son, that whoever believes in Him should not perish but have everlasting life. For God did not send His Son into the world to condemn the world, but that the world through Him might be saved. (John 3:16–17)

After the death, burial, and resurrection of Jesus and His ascension into heaven in the book of Acts, God poured out His Holy Spirit as part of His plan to build a Church—God's Church—and Jesus would be the Head of that Church, and as Christians, we would be the Body.

He is the image of the invisible God, the first-born over all creation. For by Him all things were created that are in heaven and that are on earth, visible and invisible, whether thrones or dominions or principalities or powers. All things were created through Him and for Him. And He is before all things, and in Him all things exist. And He is the head of the body, the church, who is the beginning, the firstborn from the dead, that in all things He may have the preeminence.

For it pleased the Father that in Him all the fullness should dwell, and by Him to reconcile all things to Himself, by Him, whether things on earth or things in heaven, having made peace through the blood of His cross.

And you, who once were alienated and enemies in your mind by wicked works, yet now He has reconciled in the body of His flesh through death, to present you holy, and blameless, and above reproach in His sight, if indeed you continue in the faith, grounded and steadfast, and are not moved away from the hope of the gospel which you heard, which was preached to every creature under heaven, of which I, Paul, became a minister. (Colossians 1:15–23)

Good plan, but what happened? God's people, who make up God's Church, began by obeying God and His expectations. However, down through the ages, God's Church has been recreated to look like the people and not what God intended. Paul said this would happen sooner or later. Let me repeat what Paul wrote to you and me today.

And you, who once were alienated and enemies in your mind by wicked works, yet now He has reconciled in the body of His flesh through death, to present you holy, and blameless, and above reproach in His sight, if indeed you continue in the faith, grounded and steadfast, and are not moved away from the hope of the gospel which you heard, which was preached to every creature under heaven, of which I, Paul, became a minister. (Colossians 1:21–23)

God's Church has been divided between doctrines of men, traditions, radical teachings, and people who don't even look or act like Christians. Churches do not seek to enter the "fields that are white unto harvest." There is fighting and backbiting among many brethren who won't repent and many who will not even repent of any sins.

Our task is great, but it's by God's hand that we can and will rebuild His Church. It will take a commitment, a dying to self, a hunger and thirst for the Spirit of God, a commitment to walk pure and holy, and a love that only God can provide for us to change and start the rebuilding process. We must change in order for others to see the change and the power of God, once again, released into the Body of Christ. Sounds impossible, but it's not.

The first tool we must pick up is to walk by faith. "Seeing those things that are not as though they are."

The second tool is to read and focus our thoughts on the Word of God every day. God will speak to you through His Word and give you instructions.

The third tool is to pray and fast. Ask God what is a reasonable fast for your personal life. We must come to a place of godly sorrow and forgiveness for our sin. If you don't know what your sin is, ask God, and He will show you.

The fourth tool is to deny yourself. Make God first in your life.

The fifth tool is pick up your cross every day. Crucify your old man every day so the new man that is created within you can grow and prosper.

The sixth tool is to follow Jesus every day. The Holy Spirit will teach you and lead you in all things.

This seems like an impossible task to perform if you try to do it in the flesh. God wants you to learn to walk in the Spirit and use His wisdom and knowledge to perform the work of rebuilding yourself and others. In the early church, people stepped out in love for the brethren, worshipped God daily, and taught the Word of God. The people even shared what they had so no one would have to go without. Many walked in the power of God with signs, wonders, and miracles. We must all walk in the agape love that God has given us. What is agape love? It's a "love that keeps on giving and expects nothing in return."

The Kingdom of God is available, just like it was for the early Church. We must open our hearts and pursue this walk in God's Kingdom, even while we are here on this Earth. How else can we harvest the fields that are ready to be reaped if we won't try to do what God is asking us to do right now? Let's step out in faith and see what God is going to do through each one of us.

Yes, there are two kingdoms. There is the kingdom of the ways of the world (in which we live and rely upon) and the Kingdom of God, which is the way Jesus walked. He even laid down His life for us, so that we could have His life. Jesus explained this life to Nicodemus, who was a ruler of the Jews.

> *There was a man of the Pharisees named Nicodemus, a ruler and a teacher of the Jews. This man came to Jesus by night and said to Him, "Rabbi, we know that You are a teacher come from God; for no one can do these signs that You do unless God is with him." Jesus answered and said to him, "Most assuredly, I say to you, unless one is born again, he cannot see the kingdom of God."*
>
> *Nicodemus said to Him, "How can a man be born when he is old? Can he enter a second time into his mother's womb and be born?" Jesus answered, "Most assuredly, I say to you, unless one is born of water and the Spirit, he cannot enter the kingdom of God. That which is born of the flesh is flesh, and that which is born of the Spirit is spirit. Do not marvel that I said to you, 'You must be born again.' The wind blows where it wishes, and you hear the sound of it, but cannot tell where it comes from and where it goes. So is everyone who is born of the Spirit."*
>
> *Nicodemus answered and said to Him, "How can these things be?" Jesus answered and said to him,*

"Are you the teacher of Israel, and do not know these things? Most assuredly, I say to you, we speak what we know and testify what we have seen, and you do not receive our witness. If I have told you earthly things and you do not believe, how will you believe if I tell you heavenly things? No one has ascended to heaven but He who came down from heaven, that is, the Son of Man who is in heaven. And as Moses lifted up the serpent in the wilderness, even so must the Son of Man be lifted up, that whoever believes in Him should not perish but have eternal life. For God so loved the world that He gave His only begotten Son, that whoever believes in Him should not perish but have everlasting life. For God did not send His Son into the world to condemn the world, but that the world through Him might be saved.

He who believes in Him is not condemned; but he who does not believe is condemned already, because he has not believed in the name of the only begotten Son of God. And this is the condemnation, that the light has come into the world, and men loved darkness rather than light, because their deeds were evil. For everyone practicing evil hates the light and does not come to the light, lest his deeds should be exposed. But he who does the truth comes to the light, that his deeds may be clearly seen, that they have been done in God." (John 3:1–21)

This is not some new revelation! This is just fully understanding what Jesus is speaking to Nicodemus without our worldly opinions and unbelief. Plain and simple: you cannot see or enter the Kingdom of God unless you believe that Jesus died on the cross for your sins, that He was raised from the dead so that you can be forgiven, and by believing He is the Son of God, and by receiving Him into your life. Only then you can have eternal life. However, Jesus did not stop His teaching about who He was and who you could become. Jesus also helps Thomas understand about His Kingdom and His life.

> *Let not your heart be troubled; you believe in God, believe also in Me. In My Father's house are many mansions; if it were not so, I would have told you. I go to prepare a place for you. And if I go and prepare a place for you, I will come again and receive you to Myself; that where I am, there you may be also. And where I go you know, and the way you know."*
>
> *Thomas said to Him, "Lord, we do not know where You are going, and how can we know the way?"*
>
> *Jesus said to him, "I am the way, the truth, and the life. No one comes to the Father except through Me. If you had known Me, you would have known My Father also; and from now on you know Him and have seen Him."* (John 14:1–7)

Somehow, we want to focus on the part of Jesus's teaching about Him preparing a place for us when we die or when He comes to take us home. That in itself is good news! Then Jesus continues, "I am the way, the truth, and the life. No one comes to the Father except through me."

Here is the key to understanding how we can rebuild God's Church. We are not dealing with bricks, mortar, and wood. We are dealing with the souls of men and women, whether they are saved or not saved. Our responsibility is to show them that Jesus is the way. The next chapter will enlighten us to not only the process, but the completed work of restoration. From this point forward, I suggest you get close to God and *hear what He is saying*. Let's pray.

Prayer

Father, we lift up our heart and ask You to enlighten us to Your understanding in rebuilding Your Church, Lord. We know some things, and yet possibly, we know nothing when it comes to rebuilding, but whichever way, we want what You want. We are willing to pay a price and a sacrifice to understand what Jesus taught Nicodemus and Thomas.

Please, Lord, open the eyes of our understanding that we might see with spiritual eyes as to how we can function in Your Kingdom while we are here on this Earth. Right now, we are willing to put our trust in You by faith. This may seem like a mountain to us, but You told us not to worry for we can remove mountains by faith in You, Lord. We declare our faith in You, and we thank You for everything You are about to do. Thank You, Father, in Jesus's name. Amen.

Chapter 11

The Meaning of the Word *Truth*

I will begin this chapter by looking at the word that Jesus used when He said, "I am the way, the truth, and the life. No one comes to the Father but through me" (John 14:6).

Truth used to be a common thing among Americans and people around the world, but now, it has become perverted, and lying has taken over, especially in our nation and even in some churches. The word *truth* that Jesus used in His explanation to Thomas is the Greek word *aletheia* and can simply be defined as *reality*. Jesus was speaking about the reality of His connection with God's Kingdom. Think about this. Jesus is here in His fleshly body, standing on the ground on the Earth, talking about being on this earth and God's Kingdom at the same time. Our tendency is to say, "Oh, but that was Jesus."

Jesus went about His Father's business here on Earth, and part of that business was that He anointed and sent out twelve disciples—and later, seventy-two disciples. Both groups went about doing the work of the Kingdom.

> *Then Jesus called His twelve disciples together*
> *and gave them power and authority over all demons,*
> *and to cure diseases. He sent them to preach the*
> *Kingdom of God and to heal the sick. (John 9:1–3)*

Were they successful?

> *So, they (the disciples) went out and preached that people should repent. And they cast out many demons and anointed with oil many who were sick and healed them. (Mark 6:12–13)*

Of course, they were with Jesus, and even if they were by them-selves, they could still find Him in the flesh to answer questions and receive encouragement. But what about us? What about every Christian alive today? How come we are not doing the works of Father God? I guess Jesus only wanted His disciples and apostles to do the work of God. That's what many churches teach, but it's not true! Maybe they don't understand because they have never asked God to show them the "reality or the real truth" of what is written in His Word.

After Jesus arose from the dead, He appeared to eleven of His disciples and gave them what is called the *Great Commission*. He also gave this same Commission to everyone from that point down through the ages, and it includes you and me today. Do you believe that He included you? He has given you the right in Christ Jesus to walk in the reality of the earth and God's Kingdom at the same time. Listen to the words of Jesus.

> *Later He appeared to the eleven as they sat at the table; and He rebuked their unbelief and hard-ness of heart, because they did not believe those who had seen Him after He had risen. And He said to them, "Go into all the world and preach the gospel to every creature. He who believes and is baptized will be saved; but he who does not believe will be condemned. And these signs will follow those who believe: In My name they will cast out demons; they will speak with new tongues; they will take up ser-pents; and if they drink anything deadly, it will by no means hurt them; they will lay hands on the sick, and they will recover." (Mark 16:14–18)*

Are you a believer in Christ Jesus? Is this talking about a believer like you, and are you included? Then why are so many Christians today reluctant to pursue the power of God and reach out to the lost and hurting? It's time for us to make a decision! We need to move forward in whatever it takes to move us into the reality of walking in the Kingdom of God and being in the world at the same time. If Jesus did it, so can we.

I know we can still have trouble believing because we have all been told that all this miracle stuff passed away back in the early days. Many of our church leaders say that all of that passed away when the apostles died. If that were true, why would we need the Holy Spirit in our lives today? The Holy Spirit is promised to you and me in the book of Acts.

> *Then Peter said to them, "Repent, and let every one of you be baptized in the name of Jesus Christ for the remission of sins; and you shall receive the gift of the Holy Spirit. For the promise is to you and to your children, and to all who are afar off, as many as the Lord our God will call." (Acts 2:38–39)*

"To you and to your children, and to all who are afar off, as many as the Lord our God will call." Is that clear?

We have the Great Commission that Jesus commanded, and here, we have the guarantee of the presence of the Holy Spirit to be extended throughout the generations until Jesus returns! Do you believe God is serious about the power of the gospel? Do you believe you can walk in the Kingdom here on earth?

I know I was skeptical at first, but then I began a study to prove or disapprove this reality that Jesus introduced to us. I can't deny the scriptures. It is evident to me that this is truth, and I am actively involved in pursuing this ability to walk here on earth and be in heaven at the same time. I want this life to be full time in my life!

In my pastoral ministry, I have walked in and out of this power walk or this reality in the Kingdom of God. I have received words of knowledge; I've laid hands on the sick, and they were healed; I have seen the brokenhearted healed; and I have cast out demons. Yet, it was not an everyday walk like Jesus did. Walking every day in the power of God and His Kingdom is what God is trying to awaken our spirits to understand and see the reality of His whole Church walking in this power and freedom! There are some who found this walk and minister in power ministries all over the world. God has opened the door for this power to every one of His children. All we need to do is step out and step into that lifestyle.

There used to be a phrase people would speak when a person acted like they might be too spiritual. The phrase was *"You are too heavenly-minded to be any earthly good."* I would love to be accused of that every day. I want to help people, and what better way to help them than through the power of God and the "way" of Jesus. Listen, Jesus was not only the way to the Father, but He was also the way to the God-kind of life. Walking every day with Jesus should be full of truth and full of life. This kind of life produces the righteousness that Jesus bought us through His life, but it also produces a heavenly life like Jesus enjoyed here on this Earth.

Speaking of righteousness, do you understand what righteousness is all about? I believe Paul explains it best if we will believe what he is saying. He is talking about our weakness, but the righteousness that we possess can strengthen us in Christ Jesus. We have become slaves to righteousness unto holiness.

> *For when you were slaves of sin, you were free in regard to righteousness. What fruit did you have then in the things of which you are now ashamed? For the end of those things is death. But now having been set free from sin, and having become slaves of God, you have your fruit to holiness, and the end, everlasting life. For the wages of sin is death, but the gift of God is eternal life in Christ Jesus our Lord.*
> (Romans 6:20–23)

You no longer have to be slaves to uncleanness, lawlessness, and even more lawlessness. Paul explains in verse 19.

> *I speak in human terms because of the weakness of your flesh. For just as you presented your members as slaves of uncleanness, and of lawlessness leading to more lawlessness, so now present your members as slaves of righteousness for holiness.* (Romans 6:19)

Listen, you and I cannot live in this world with all its impossibilities and not have the power of God to strengthen us and empower us to do His work. Even Jesus is still available to work with us when we step out in faith and minister to the world around us.

> *So then, after the Lord had spoken to them, He was received up into heaven, and sat down at the right hand of God. And they went out and preached everywhere, the Lord working with them and confirming the word through the accompanying signs. Amen.* (Mark 16:19–20)

When we as Christians get our lives in God's order, then God's Church will automatically come into order. God is waiting on us!

You are a redeemed person through Christ Jesus. You no longer must live a life empowered by the flesh and the sin of this world. You are free to walk in holiness. You literally need to see yourself alive unto Christ Jesus! He is your model and your life! Freedom belongs to you!

> *I can do all things through Christ who strengthens me."* (Philippians 4:13)

It's you and Jesus working together that can rebuild God's Church, one Christian at a time! Begin to thank God that He has called you to such a time as this.

Chapter 12

What Is Our Individual Plan?

Now, we are down to the critical part of the book. God has explained His desire for us to rebuild. He has given us instructions to prepare ourselves and how to function in rebuilding, and He has backed up everything by His Word. The question is, "What are you going to do about God's Church in ruins? You, personally, what is your plan to get started on this task God has given you? How are you going to prepare yourself to walk daily with God in His Kingdom?

Maybe your response is, "I will have to wait until I can see how things progress," or "Let me see when I will have time to start the process of repentance and prayer." Or "I have things I need to do first, and when I finish, maybe I will have time then." What does God think about our putting things off?

> *Come now, you who say, "Today or tomorrow we will go to such and such a city, spend a year there, buy and sell, and make a profit." Whereas you do not know what will happen tomorrow. For what is your life? It is even a vapor that appears for a little time and then vanishes away. Instead, you ought to say, "If the Lord wills, we shall live and do this or that." But now you boast in your arrogance. All such boasting is evil. Therefore, to him who knows to do*

good and does not do it, to him it is sin. (James 4:13–17)

Remember, God knows our heart and what we think on the inside. God is not calling you to die; He's calling you to live the way He created you to live! God wants to see each one of us as Christians to be able to fulfill what He has called us to be. Remember what the word "Christian" means? It means "to be like Christ!"

How can we measure our lives as being like Christ if we allow the world to be our every influence? How can we love like Jesus when most of us don't possess that kind of love? We have the love of the world, but much of this is lust and not love. God called it "the lust of the eyes, the lust of the flesh, and the boastful pride of life." Jesus resisted the temptations of the flesh and the world, and so can we.

Another excuse would be, "I don't have the time to make changes. I'm too busy living my life." That mentality is right up there with denying God! Jesus told us we are to deny ourselves! The problem is that we have become used to the life in the world, and we don't want to give it up. So the time of decision is here. Do you want to follow the world or Jesus?

> *Then Jesus said to His disciples, "If anyone desires to come after Me, let him deny himself, and take up his cross, and follow Me. For whoever desires to save his life will lose it, but whoever loses his life for My sake will find it. For what profit is it to a man if he gains the whole world, and loses his own soul? Or what will a man give in exchange for his soul? For the Son of Man will come in the glory of His Father with His angels, and then He will reward each according to his works."* (Matthew 16:24–27)

Denying yourself and taking up your cross is not difficult. It's a daily decision to make the right choices in your relationship with God. You lay down your life, and you put to death (or take up your cross) to put sin out of your life, and you choose to follow God every day for the rest of your life on Earth or until Jesus returns.

Jesus said, "Follow me!" To follow Jesus is not a suggestion; it is a command, just like when Jesus gave the Great Commission. He commanded us to "go ye therefore and preach the Gospel" And we are to obey! Once again, here is the scripture support.

> *And He said to them, "Go into all the world and preach the gospel to every creature. He who believes and is baptized will be saved; but he who does not believe will be condemned. And these signs will follow those who believe: In My name they will cast out demons; they will speak with new tongues; they will take up serpents; and if they drink anything deadly, it will by no means hurt them; they will lay hands on the sick, and they will recover."*
> (Mark 16:15–18)

If you are truly a Christian, then you should have a burning desire in your heart to work with God to rebuild His Church! You might say, "I know, but I don't know how." Scripture says you already have the answer in your spirit.

> *I can do all things through Christ who strengthens me.* (Philippians 4:13)

Just think of the power you possess by being a Christian and how much power all Christians could have if we would band together in unity and love and set out to do the work!

Why is God so determined to rebuild His Church anyway? Can't He do it without me? Absolutely! But you may not like the reward you will obtain. Listen, we are in the end-times, and God is going to send Jesus, the Bridegroom, to come and take His Bride, "who is without spot or wrinkle."

But how do I know that I will even be here when that happens? That's not the real issue. The real issue is what's going to happen if you are still here? God is attempting to *"wake up"* the Body of Christ to be ready when that day comes. In the meantime, there is work to be done.

If we are still here before Jesus comes, then you need to read the book of Revelation to see how hell is released into the world, especially against the Christians. If you have not read this last book of the Bible, I suggest you take time right now to read and study what is out in the future that we might be a part of.

This is the reason that God wants to restore and rebuild the Body of Christ. God loves you, and He wants you to be able to stand and continue declaring the Word of the Lord until Jesus comes in the sky. Do you understand this perspective? Right now, we are moving into the greatest work of grace that Christians have ever seen.

So our individual plan should start with making sure we are on solid ground with God the Father. This comes through prayer and any repentance that needs to take place. Remember, God wants us to be holy and pure. You need to ask God if there is any sin in your life or any hidden sin you have not dealt with. Is there any unforgiveness or have you lost your ability to love like Jesus loves? All these things are hindrances to walking in God's way and God's power.

The next area is hunger. Do you have a hunger in your heart for more of God, more of His power, more of the depth of His love, and more of grace and mercy? Jesus said you are blessed when you have a hunger in your heart.

Blessed are those who hunger and thirst for righteousness, for they shall be filled. (Matthew 5:6)

Hunger is a natural part of our human body. But Jesus is talking about a deeper hunger that goes down into our spirit and cannot be satisfied. This is one of the characteristics that indicates how much we want to see God's Glory and move in an outpouring of the Holy Spirit in God's Church today. Only God can satisfy this hunger.

There is another thing that is really important as we seek God in this task. We need to change our way of thinking. We have allowed ourselves to think according to the influence of this world, and it is all messed up. Example: When you get sick, what is the first thing you think about? You think you need some medicine, and/or you need to go to the doctor.

We should be in a position right now that we no longer think about things the way the world does. We are to think the way Jesus thought by allowing us to learn and hear from God and attend the sickness of the world through faith in God.

> *Be anxious for nothing, but in everything by prayer and supplication, with thanksgiving, let your requests be made known to God; and the peace of God, which surpasses all understanding, will guard your hearts and minds through Christ Jesus.*
>
> *Finally, brethren, whatever things are true, whatever things are noble, whatever things are just, whatever things are pure, whatever things are lovely, whatever things are of good report, if there is any virtue and if there is anything praiseworthy, meditate on these things. The things which you learned and received and heard and saw in me, these do, and the God of peace will be with you.* (Philippians 4:6–9)

Paul then calls out to the church at Rome that they take heed as to how they live their lives and how they think and talk. He calls this aspect of our lives "our reasonable service." You will find it in the verse below. Then he calls us to renew our mind. He didn't say daily, but I believe this reasonable service is something that we do every day.

> *I beseech you therefore, brethren, by the mercies of God, that you present your bodies a living sacrifice, holy, acceptable to God, which is your reasonable service.*
>
> *And do not be conformed to this world, but be transformed by the renewing of your mind, that*

*you may prove what is that good and acceptable and
perfect will of God.* (Romans 12:1–2)

Throughout this writing, I have used the word "faith" over and over and over. We cannot live without faith in God and be who God called us to be. I'm an advocate of common sense, but when it comes to faith, you can't live in God's Kingdom without it! Listen to this statement: *God can't multiply back to you if you haven't trusted Him for anything.*

God lives by sowing and reaping. He expects us to do the same thing. If we never sow a seed from our life, then there is no way we can expect a harvest or any kind of return. Jesus spoke this way of living when He talked about giving.

> *Judge not, and you shall not be judged. Condemn not, and you shall not be condemned. Forgive, and you will be forgiven. Give, and it will be given to you: good measure, pressed down, shaken together, and running over will be put into your bosom. For with the same measure that you use, it will be measured back to you.* (Luke 6:37–38)

Giving freely comes from a heart who loves like God loves. We don't judge someone or something by what we think or maybe even see. We give because God said to give, and He will bless us. I cannot number the gifts God has poured out on me and my family because of our giving freely. It is totally amazing, and no one can convince you to see this unless you practice sowing yourself.

> *A good man out of the good treasure of his heart brings forth good; and an evil man out of the evil treasure of his heart brings forth evil. For out of the abundance of the heart his mouth speaks.* (Luke 6:45)

So it's time to step off the cliff into the unknown. This part of our future is going to be a learning experience and a solid confirmation that we belong to God. Please don't let the enemy sidetrack you. Instead, make every day your day of victory by placing the devil under your feet!

One final thought. How will we know that God's Church has been rebuilt and restored? It's very simple.

> *Go into all the world and preach the gospel to every creature. He who believes and is baptized will be saved; but he who does not believe will be condemned. And these signs will follow those who believe: In My name they will cast out demons; they will speak with new tongues; they will take up serpents; and if they drink anything deadly, it will by no means hurt them; they will lay hands on the sick, and they will recover. (Mark 16:15–18)*

> *And they went out and preached everywhere, the Lord working with them and confirming the word through the accompanying signs. (Mark 16:20)*

So pick up your sword—the sword of the Holy Spirit—and your shield of faith. Let the enemy know that you mean business! God bless you as you walk in the wonders of God's Kingdom. I pray that God continues to restore you, refresh you, and revive you as you live each day with your eyes focused on Jehovah God!

Work has started. The flame of God is still burning. Let's rebuild His Church to contain the fulness of His Fire and His Glory! Let's see the abundance of His Harvest come in quickly and in a short amount of time.

Conclusion

Here, we are at the end of this God-inspired book on *Rebuilding God's Church*. It seems like it has been a long journey, but in "reality," it is not! I have been faithful in writing what God has instructed me to write, and now, I join with "you, the Christian people" in walking out God's instructions and His desire.

I ask that you stop and consider with an open heart just how far our nation has fallen in the last two years. This is just one more sign that we are in the last days, according to the wisdom of Jesus. We must "gird up our loins" and move forward in defeating the darkness while rebuilding the lives of Christians who make up God's Church. Just remember that miracles are common practice for God and His Kingdom, and they are signs for the unbelievers. The devil is our enemy, and he will stop at nothing to tear down and destroy what we rebuild. But take heart; like Jesus, we have overcome the works of the devil, and we stand firm in the offensive position. We are the winners, and we have the victory!

For a season, I have stood with intercessors across the United States in tearing down the strongholds, the principalities, the powers, the rulers of darkness, and spiritual wickedness in high places. Each day, we stand in prayer, defeating and binding this blatant enemy. We stand on the promise from God that "whatsoever we bind here on earth, God will bind in heaven."

> *And I also say to you that you are Peter, and on this rock, I will build My church, and the gates of Hades shall not prevail [overpower] against it. And*

I will give you the keys of the kingdom of heaven, and whatever you bind on earth will be bound in heaven, and whatever you loose on earth will be loosed in heaven. (Matthew 16:18–19)

The Greek Word *katischusousin* is translated to "prevail or to overcome."

So as we stand in victory, let us also stand in peace. God has given us a peace that far surpasses the peace that the world claims. Jesus repeats what He has heard the Father say.

Peace, I leave with you, My peace I give to you; not as the world gives do I give to you. Let not your heart be troubled, neither let it be afraid. (John 14:26–27)

Keep the oil of God ever present in your life and be filled with the fire of God as you pursue this calling. With the oil, your fire will not go out! Keep walking with the Holy Spirit each day as well. God bless you! I pray that God will continue to restore, refresh, and revive you as you walk with Him.

Here, in February 2023, God set down in Asbury University, located in Wilmore, Kentucky. God came down in response to a few students that had a hunger and a thirst for the Holy Spirit to bring revival to their school. After several weeks of round-the-clock prayer, fasting, and worship, revival set down in the school.

People from around the world began to respond with their presence. God began to touch other areas in our nation and around the world. This is the result of repentance and hunger! As of the time of writing this manuscript, the revival is still active and spreading! Keep the fire burning! Keep the oil of the Holy Spirit available for the fire! Reach out and receive all that God is doing! This is the most powerful way to rebuild God's Church!

About the Author

Dallas Wauson has been in the pastoral ministry for forty years. He has pastored three churches, the last being River of Life Church in Eagle Pass, Texas. He has a passion for awakening in our nation and all over the world. Walking in the way of Jesus is so important right now, and it's for the church to wake up. Jesus understands the people that struggle with selling out to Jesus and remain under the influence of the flesh. To see the difference in God's Church and the church that man has created, God has called this pastor to intervene in this critical time for God's Church.